Iron Deficiency Anemia Cookbook

The Ultimate Guide to Overcoming Iron Deficiency Anemia through Nourishing Recipes

Isabella Reynolds

Contents

About the Author

Isabella Reynolds is an accomplished author, passionate cook, and advocate for healthy living. She has authored a book titled "Iron Deficiency Anemia Cookbook." The book aims to demystify and combat iron deficiency anemia, offering not only delectable recipes but also comprehensive guidance on managing and preventing the condition.

Also, Isabella's multicultural background and family culinary traditions inspired her love for cooking, which she combined with her expertise in nutrition to create nourishing and delicious recipes tailored to individuals with iron deficiency anemia. She is dedicated to simplifying complex concepts and providing practical guidance to her readers.

Isabella actively collaborates with medical professionals and organizations to raise awareness about iron deficiency anemia. Through her book and efforts, she seeks to empower individuals with the knowledge and tools they need to make informed decisions about their health.

Introduction

The "Iron Deficiency Anemia Cookbook" is a culinary guide that aims to restore vitality and combat the challenges of iron deficiency anemia. This common condition can cause fatigue and weakness, but this cookbook offers a collection of delicious and nourishing recipes rich in iron. With a focus on flavour and nutrition, the book provides meals that replenish iron stores while exciting the taste buds.

It also provides knowledge on iron-rich foods, optimal combinations, and absorption-enhancing cooking techniques. Whether you're a beginner or an experienced chef, this cookbook empowers you to take charge of your health through the healing power of food. By adopting a culinary approach rooted in both science and pleasure, you can reclaim vitality and savour the joy of eating while supporting your body's iron requirements.

Let this cookbook be your guide on the journey to optimal health.

Understanding Iron Deficiency Anemia

To overcome anemia, nourishing recipes could be your best bet. But you must bear in mind that you need to understand the basics of iron deficiency anemia. Because the easiest way to solve a problem is to acknowledge the problem.

Therefore, you will learn about iron deficiency anemia, its causes, symptoms, diagnosis, and treatment in this chapter. That alone will equip you with the necessary details about this disease. Now, let's unravel the basics of iron deficiency anemia.

What is Iron Deficiency Anemia?

Iron deficiency anemia is a condition that occurs when there is a lack of iron in the body, leading to a decrease in the production of hemoglobin. Hemoglobin is a protein found in red blood cells that carries oxygen from the lungs to the rest of the body.

In addition, iron is an essential mineral that is required for the body to produce hemoglobin. When there is insufficient iron, the body is unable to make enough hemoglobin, resulting in a reduced ability to transport oxygen. Consequently, the symptoms of iron deficiency anemia start manifesting.

Risk Factors for Iron Deficiency Anemia

A lot of risk factors can aggravate the chances of developing iron deficiency anemia. However, they don't necessarily guarantee its occurrence.

In this subsection, I will be sharing with you some risk factors you need to pay attention to:

Inadequate Iron Intake: A diet that lacks sufficient iron-rich foods can increase the risk of developing iron deficiency anemia. This is especially true for individuals who follow restrictive diets, such as vegetarians or vegans, as plant-based sources of iron are less readily absorbed by the body.

Blood Loss: Any condition that leads to chronic blood loss can result in iron deficiency anemia. Examples include gastrointestinal conditions like ulcers, gastritis, colon polyps, or inflammatory bowel disease, as well as heavy menstrual periods in women.

Pregnancy and Breastfeeding: Pregnant and breastfeeding women require increased amounts of iron to support the growth and development of the fetus and to compensate for iron loss during breastfeeding. Insufficient iron intake or inadequate supplementation during these periods can contribute to iron deficiency anemia.

Rapid Growth and Development: Infants, children, and adolescents experience periods of rapid growth, during which their iron requirements increase. If their dietary iron intake is insufficient to meet these increased demands, iron deficiency anemia may occur.

Gastrointestinal Disorders: Certain gastrointestinal disorders can interfere with the absorption of iron. These include celiac disease, Crohn's disease, and gastric bypass surgery. In these conditions, your body may struggle to absorb iron from the diet, leading to iron deficiency anemia over time.

Chronic Kidney Disease: Individuals with chronic kidney disease are at a higher risk of developing iron deficiency anemia. This is partly due to decreased production of erythropoietin, a hormone that stimulates red blood cell production and iron absorption.

Chronic Diseases and Inflammation: Chronic inflammatory conditions such as rheumatoid arthritis, lupus, or chronic infections can affect iron metabolism and lead to iron deficiency anemia.

Age: Infants, young children, and older adults may be at higher risk of iron deficiency anemia due to their specific nutritional needs and potential factors like poor dietary habits or underlying medical conditions.

Causes and Symptoms

The focus of this subsection is to let you know the likely causes and symptoms of iron deficiency anemia. Therefore, you should pay attention to the details I want to share with you here. With these details, you will know what to abstain from to prevent the occurrence of iron deficiency anemia. Not only that, you will also know the appropriate time to consult a healthcare professional.

Causes of Iron Deficiency Anemia

Now, let's talk about the causes of iron deficiency anemia.

- Inadequate Iron Intake

- Blood Loss

- Poor Iron Absorption: Certain conditions can impair the absorption of iron from the diet. Examples include celiac disease, inflammatory bowel disease, gastric bypass surgery, or other gastrointestinal disorders that affect the small intestine's ability to absorb nutrients effectively.

- Increased Iron Requirements: During periods of rapid growth and development, such as infancy, childhood, adolescence, and pregnancy, the body requires more iron. If the increased iron needs are not met through diet or supplementation, iron deficiency anemia can occur.

Having talked about the causes. The next thing you want to know is the symptoms of iron deficiency anemia.

Symptoms of Iron Deficiency Anemia

The symptoms of iron deficiency anemia can vary in severity and may not always be specific to iron deficiency anemia. Here are some of its symptoms:

- Fatigue and Weakness
- Shortness of Breath
- Rapid or Irregular Heartbeat
- Headaches and Dizziness
- Cold Hands and Feet
- Abnormal cravings for non-food items such as clay, ice, or dirt.

Diagnosis and Treatment

To diagnose iron deficiency anemia, healthcare professionals typically perform the following assessments:

- Medical history
- Physical examination
- Blood tests (such as CBC, serum ferritin, and transferrin saturation).

Treatment of iron deficiency anemia typically includes;

- Iron supplementation
- Dietary modifications
- Addressing underlying causes
- Blood transfusion or intravenous iron therapy (in severe cases).

In conclusion, you need to understand the concept of iron deficiency anemia. It is from the knowledge that you can manage the ailment. And in the next chapter, I will explain in detail how you can manage anemia effectively using the right strategies.

General Guide for Managing Anemia

Managing anemia is one thing you shouldn't compromise. If you allow it to aggravate beyond control, it could open the door to numerous deadly diseases. Therefore, I will provide you with a viable guide for managing anemia in this chapter.

You will learn about the essence of balanced diets in managing anemia. In the subsequent subsection, I will give you a list of foods that can help you treat anemia. In addition, you will learn about enhancing iron absorption and necessary nutrients and supplements for anemia.

We have a lot to unravel in this chapter. So, let's get into the details.

Importance of a Balance Diet

A balanced diet is all you need when it comes to managing anemia! This is because a balanced diet provides the essential nutrients needed to combat anemia and boost your energy levels. Iron-rich foods like spinach and beans act as powerful allies, while vitamin C swoops in to help absorb that iron.

You also need to bear in mind that vitamin B12 and folate team up to keep your red blood cells strong. By fueling your body with a diverse range of nutritious foods, you'll be ready to fight anemia and feel like a true superhero! After all, regaining healthy living is a battle, and no battle or struggle is small.

In essence, you will agree with me that balanced diets play a significant role in managing anemia.

Foods that Treat Anemia

To treat anemia, incorporating specific foods into your diet can make a significant difference. Iron-rich foods like meats, seafood, legumes, and leafy greens help combat iron-deficiency anemia.

Also, foods high in vitamin C, such as citrus fruits and tomatoes, help in iron absorption. Vitamin B12 sources like beef liver, eggs, and dairy products are beneficial for B12-deficiency anemia. Folate-rich foods like leafy greens and legumes address folate-deficiency anemia.

You also need to include foods rich in vitamin A, vitamin E, and copper to support red blood cell production. And always remember that you still need to consult a healthcare professional for personalized advice.

Enhancing Iron Absorption

Enhancing iron absorption is crucial if you are struggling against anemia or looking to optimize your iron levels. I have prepared brief explanations of some effective strategies to improve your iron absorption:

- Pair iron-rich foods with vitamin C sources like citrus fruits, bell peppers, and broccoli to improve iron absorption.

- Avoid consuming calcium-rich foods and beverages like dairy products, tea, and coffee during meals with iron-rich foods, as they can inhibit iron absorption.

- Cooking acidic foods in cast iron cookware can increase the iron content of the meal, but this method shouldn't be relied upon as the sole means of boosting iron absorption.

- Soaking legumes, grains, and seeds before cooking, as well as incorporating fermented foods, can help reduce compounds that hinder iron absorption.

- Be mindful of excessive fiber consumption with iron-rich meals, as high-fiber foods can reduce iron absorption. Therefore, you have to ensure that you space out such consumption throughout the day.

- If prescribed iron supplements, follow the healthcare professional's instructions and consider taking them with vitamin C-rich foods to enhance absorption.

Nutrients and Supplements for Anemia

When addressing anemia, certain nutrients and supplements can be beneficial for improving blood health. However, you can equally do well to consult a registered dietitian or a healthcare professional for nutrient and supplement recommendations.

Although I have some key ones you can check out:

- Iron: Iron supplements or iron-rich foods such as lean meats, seafood, legumes, spinach, and fortified cereals can help replenish iron levels.

- Vitamin C: Consuming vitamin C alongside iron-rich foods or supplements enhances iron absorption. Strawberries, citrus fruits, tomatoes, and bell peppers are all rich in vitamin C. Therefore, you should take them as much as you can.

- Vitamin B12: If you have vitamin B12 deficiency anemia, supplements or foods like beef liver, fish, eggs, and dairy products can provide the necessary B12.

- Folate (Vitamin B9): Folate plays a vital role in red blood cell production. Leafy greens, legumes, asparagus, and fortified grains are good sources of folate.

- Vitamin A: Vitamin A supports red blood cell development. Foods like carrots, sweet potatoes, spinach, and apricots contain vitamin A.

- Vitamin E: Vitamin E helps protect red blood cells from damage. So, you should always take nuts, broccoli, seeds, and spinach as they are rich in vitamin E.

- Copper: Copper is essential for iron absorption and red blood cell production. Shellfish, organ meats, seeds, nuts, and dark chocolate are good sources of copper.

- Vitamin D: Adequate vitamin D levels support healthy red blood cell production. Sun exposure and fortified dairy products can help increase vitamin D intake.

In short, the whole chapter focuses on the effective ways of managing anemia. I estimate that you must have picked some vital information. But don't forget you still need to consult either a registered dietitian or a healthcare professional for proper guidance on how to go about your diets, nutrients, and supplements to manage anemia better.

Conclusion

In conclusion, the "Iron Deficiency Anemia Cookbook" serves as a valuable resource for individuals seeking to understand and manage this common condition. By providing a comprehensive understanding of iron deficiency anemia, you should be empowered with the knowledge to make informed decisions about your health. The general guide for managing anemia equips you with practical strategies and a wide array of delicious recipes to incorporate into your daily lives.

With this cookbook, you can embark on a transformative culinary journey that not only satisfies your taste buds but also replenishes your iron stores. From iron-rich ingredients to clever combinations and innovative cooking techniques, this cookbook demonstrates that managing anemia doesn't mean compromising on flavour or enjoyment.

By following the recipes and guidelines presented, you can embrace a balanced and nutritious diet that supports the production of healthy red blood cells. With each meal, you will nourish your body, boost your energy levels, and ultimately overcome the challenges posed by iron deficiency anemia.

The "Iron Deficiency Anemia Cookbook" is more than just a collection of recipes; it is a powerful tool that empowers you to take charge of your health and transform your relationship with food. Through its pages, you will discover that managing anemia can be a journey of culinary exploration, self-care, and renewed vitality.

So, grab your apron, sharpen your knives, and dive into the world of vibrant flavours and nutrient-rich dishes. Let the "Iron Deficiency Anemia Cookbook" be your trusted companion on the path to optimal health and well-being. Bear in mind that with each bite, you are nourishing not only your body but also your journey towards a vibrant and iron-rich life.

I wish you good luck!

Iron Rich Smoothie

Are you looking for a tasty way to increase your iron level? Try this iron rich smoothie which is not only healthy but is also tastes heavenly to start your day with.

Prep Time: 15 min   Cook Time: 00 mins   Servings: 2

Ingredients:

225 ml orange juice (1 cup)	1 ripe kiwi
1 frozen banana	15g blackstrap molasses (1 tbsp)
2 handfuls baby spinach	
14 g cacao powder (2 tbsp)	
1 pitted or prune date	
28 g unsalted raw pumpkin seeds (2 tbsp)	

Instructions:

1. Take a blender and combine banana, kiwi, orange juice, cocoa powder, spinach, pumpkin seeds, and molasses.
2. Blend all the ingredients for thirty seconds or till everything is fully combined and have a creamy consistency.
3. Serve.

Nutritional Values:

Calories: 257 g, Fat: 5.4 g, Carbs: 53.3 g, Protein: 6.4 g, Iron: 3.5 mg

Tropical Green Smoothie

This delicious smoothie is packed with richness of iron and is known to be best to fight anemia. With all the goodness this smoothie is perfect for breakfast or for anyone who is having low iron in their bodies.

Prep Time: 02 min   **Cook Time: 00 mins**   **Servings: 2**

Ingredients:

1 lemon juiced	240 g washed baby spinach (2 cups)
227 g iced water (8 oz)	
1 peeled mandarin orange	
240 g pineapple (1 cup)	
120 ml orange juice (1/2 cup)	
240 g stem removed kale (2 cups)	

Instructions:

1. Take a blender and put all the ingredients in it.
2. Start blending the ingredients for two mins or till it has reached smooth consistency.
3. Enjoy!

Nutritional Values:

Calories: 271 g, Fat: 2 g, Carbs: 62 g, Protein: 10 g, Iron: 4 mg

Strawberry Banana Smoothie

This smoothie is perfect for people suffering from anemia. As all the iron rich fruits are blended into almond milk.

Prep Time: 03 min   **Cook Time: 00 mins**   **Servings: 2**

Ingredients:

280 g strawberries (10 oz)	30 ml lemon juice (2 tbsp)
60 ml organic honey (1/4 cup)	
1 peeled and sliced banana	
340 g soft tofu (12 oz)	
240 ml almond milk (1 cup)	
A pinch of salt	

Instructions:

1. Take a blender and blend all the ingredients till you reach desired consistency.
2. Pour the smoothie into the glass and ENJOY!

Nutritional Values:

Calories: 214 g, Fat: 4.3 g, Carbs: 39.5 g, Protein: 9.4 g, Iron: 3.5 mg

Anemia Fighting Smoothie

If you are fighting with stress, anxiety or depression try our anemia fighting smoothie. This healthy smoothie is high in iron and Vitamin C plus it is made in no time.

Prep Time: 03 min   **Cook Time: 00 mins**   **Servings: 1**

Ingredients:

480 ml fresh baby power greens (2 cups)	240 ml cold water (1 cup)
1 handful ice	
75 g green grapes (1/2 cup)	
1 peeled lemon wedge	
½ peeled kiwi	
Stevia or any other sweetener	

Instructions:

1. Take lemon and kiwi and peel them off. Add lemon and kiwi into the blender.
2. Then add rest of the ingredients and blend till the consistency is smooth.

Nutritional Values:

Calories: 89 g, Fat: 0.6 g, Carbs: 21.5 g, Protein: 2.7 g, Iron: 2 mg

All-Natural Smoothie Bowl

This smoothie bowl is made using vegetables and fruits which are naturally high in iron.

Prep Time: 10 min   Cook Time: 00 mins   Servings: 2

Ingredients:

80 g raw pepitas (1/2 cup)	10 g maca powder (2 tsp)
15 g cacao powder (1 tbsp)	210 g fresh spinach (3 cups)
2 bananas	480 ml unsweetened coconut water (2 cups)
140 g frozen cherries (1 cup)	
Homemade protein powder	
140 g frozen strawberries (1 cup)	

Instructions:

1. Add coconut water, pepitas and spinach into a clean blender.
2. Blend till you have reached the desired consistency.
3. Then add all the other ingredients and blend till its smooth.

Nutritional Values:

Calories: 338 g, Fat: 10 g, Carbs: 60 g, Protein:12 g, Iron: 5 mg

Cherry Cacao Smoothie

This iron boosting smoothie is full flavours. The tang and sweet flavours of cherries beautifully compliments the chocolatey flavour of cacao powder.

Prep Time: 05 min   Cook Time: 00 mins   Servings: 1

Ingredients:

180 ml unsweetened milk of your choice (3/4 cup)	0.25 g camu camu powder (1/4 tsp)
1 scoop of protein powder or collagen peptides	150 g pre pitted frozen cherries (3/4 cup)
60 ml leafy greens (1/4 cup)	
16 g cacao powder (2 g)	
16 g cashew butter (1 tbsp)	
2 pitted medjool dates	

Instructions:

1. Make sure that dates and cherries do not have any pits.
2. Add all the ingredients into the blender.
3. Blend all the ingredients at high speed for few mins.
4. Pour the smoothie into a glass and enjoy.

Nutritional Values:

Calories: 475 g, Fat: 9.5 g, Carbs: 50 g, Protein: 15 g, Iron: 4 mg

Breakfast Slice

This versatile recipe is perfect for breakfast, snack or even as a tasty dessert. This slice is combination of iron rich food like cashew, quinoa, and sesame seeds.

Prep Time: 10 min   Cook Time: 40 mins   Servings: 12

Ingredients:

140 g pumpkin seeds (1 cup)	90 g oats (1 cup)
2 bananas	60 ml chocolate chips (1/4 cup)
15 ml vanilla extract (1 tbsp)	140 g sesame seeds (1 cup)
140 g quinoa flakes (1 cup)	140 g almonds (1 cup)
60 ml maple syrup (1 tbsp)	
140 g cashews (1 cup)	

Instructions:

1. Before doing anything else preheat your oven at 180 Degrees C. with the help of baking paper line the baking dish.
2. In a blender process all the seeds and nuts till a coarse meal is formed.
3. Now add maple syrup, banana and vanilla. Blend everything till it is fully combined.
4. Add chocolate chips to the mixture.
5. Spread the mix on the baking tray.
6. Smooth the mixture using spoon.
7. Bake it for forty mins till the top is browned.
8. Make slices of it and enjoy.

Nutritional Values:

Calories: 318 g, Fat: 19 g, Carbs: 22 g, Protein: 10.4 g, Iron: 2.74 mg

Vegan Pineapple & Coconut Baked Oatmeal

Enjoy this delicious vegan oatmeal which is full of tropical flavours and is easiest to make. It's the perfect family breakfast which is fulfilling and healthy.

Prep Time: 15 min　　　**Cook Time: 50 mins**　　　**Servings: 6**

Ingredients:

80 g toasted unsweetened shredded coconut	3.5 g ground cinnamon (1 ½ tsp)
480 ml unsweetened non-dairy milk (2 cups)	120 ml pure maple syrup (1/2 cup)
180 g non-dairy yogurt (3/4 cup)	28 g coconut oil (2 tbsp)
5 ml vanilla extract (1 tsp)	4 g baking powder (1 tsp)
340 g diced pineapples (2 cups)	200 g rolled oats (2 cups)
4.5 g salt (3/4 tsp)	

Instructions:

1. Before doing anything else preheat the oven at 180 Degree F. Take a square baking dish and coat it with cooking spray.
2. Take a bowl and mix all the ingredients into a bowl. Make sure everything is combined well.
3. Now pour the mixture to the baking dish and bake for fifty mins till the top has turned golden and is firm when touched

Nutritional Values:

Calories: 488 g, Fat: 29 g, Carbs: 55 g, Protein: 7 g, Iron: 5 mg

Eggs, Sriracha & Avocado Overnight Oats

If you love avocados, this recipe is a must-try for you. This healthy and delicious recipe can be made with just a few ingredients and easy steps.

Prep Time: 15 min   **Cook Time: 00 mins**   **Servings:**

Ingredients:

45 g oats (1/2 cup)	15 g onion (1tbsp)
5 ml sriracha (1 tsp)	180 ml water (3/4 cup)
30 g chopped cherry tomatoes (2 tomatoes)	1 fried egg
25 g sliced avocado (1/2 avocado)	

Instructions:

1. Take jar or bowl and mix oats and water together. Cover container you choose and refrigerate it overnight.
2. Add onion to the oats then microwave the bowl for thirty seconds intervals, stir the ingredients occasionally till everything is heated through.
3. Now add tomatoes and avocados to the bowl then top it with sriracha and fried egg.

Nutritional Values:

Calories: 317 g, Fat: 15 g, Carbs: 35 g, Protein: 13 g, Iron: 0.4 mg

Chia Pudding

This healthy chia pudding is what we have been craving for. Be it a quick breakfast or a healthy snack its good for anytime of the day.

Prep Time: 10 min   Cook Time: 10 mins   Servings: 4

Ingredients:

400 ml coconut milk (13.5 oz)	1 sliced banana
1.25 g salt (1/4 tsp)	Toasted walnuts and banana slices, to serve
15 ml vanilla extract (1 tbsp)	4-5 dates
35 g chia seeds (1/4 cup)	10 g cinnamon (2 tsp)

Instructions:

1. Take a blender and put all the ingredients in it, start blending the ingredients even everything get smooth.
2. Spread the mixture into four jars and cover them with lid.
3. Refrigerate the mixture overnight.
4. Next day top the mixture with toasted walnuts and banana slices.
5. Enjoy.

Nutritional Values:

Calories: 312 g, Fat: 25 g, Carbs: 21 g, Protein: 4 g, Iron: 4 mg

Green Smoothie for Anemia

Spinach is known to be a great source of iron and this green recipe have good amount of spinach in it. Furthermore, this recipe is not only good for boosting your iron intake but also helps your providing other health benefits like it's good for eye health and also helps in lowering the risk of stroke, cancer and many other serious conditions.

Prep Time: 05 min   **Cook Time: 00 mins**   **Servings: 2**

Ingredients:

30 g pumpkin seeds (2 tbsp)	30 g spinach (1 cup)
130 g orange (1)	
160 g watermelon (1 cup)	
60 g banana (1/2)	
30 g kale (1/2 cup)	

Instructions:

1. Put all the ingredients in a blender.
2. Process the ingredients for two mins, add water if necessary.
3. Pour the smoothie in serving glass and enjoy.

Nutritional Values:

Calories: 291 g, Fat: 10g, Carbs: 47 g, Protein: 11 g, Iron: 4.9 mg

Dark Chocolate Smoothie

This is a simple but delicious iron smoothie recipe with only four ingredients. It is not only healthful, but it will also satisfy your sweet tooth. It also contains a substance called as lauric acid, which helps in the maintenance of your immune system's strength.

Prep Time: 03 min   **Cook Time: 00 mins**   **Servings: 1**

Ingredients:

120 g banana (1)	
28 g cocoa powder or dark chocolate (1 oz)	
120 ml coconut milk (1/2 cup)	
28 g almonds (1 oz)	

Instructions:

1. Take a blender and add all of your ingredients in it.
2. Add one cup of ice then blend for two mins.
3. Blend till you reach the desired consistency and then pour it in glass.
4. Enjoy!

Nutritional Values:

Calories: 530 g, Fat: 38 g, Carbs: 42 g, Protein: 10 g, Iron: 4.4 mg

Kale & Parsley Iron Smoothie

Iron-rich foods include kale, parsley, and flaxseeds. Oranges, strawberries, and limes, on the other hand, are high in vitamin C, which can help with iron absorption. Parsley also has powerful anti-inflammatory effects. It is high in antioxidants such as vitamins A, C, E, all of which have been shown to decrease inflammation.

Prep Time: 05 min   Cook Time: 00 mins   Servings: 2

Ingredients:

15 g parsley (1/2 cup)	67 g kale (1 cup)
130 g orange (1)	120 g banana (1)
10 g flaxseed (1tbsp)	
67 g lime (1)	
75 g strawberries (1/2 cup)	

Instructions:

1. Firstly, juice the lemon and orange.
2. Then add the juices along with other ingredients in a blender.
3. Blend for two mins till everything is full combined.
4. Serve immediately & enjoy.

Nutritional Values:

Calories: 308 g, Fat: 5 g, Carbs: 66 g, Protein: 8 g, Iron: 4 mg

Lentil Smoothie

If you're a vegetarian or vegan, it's critical that you receive adequate protein from plants. Why not try a tasty lentil smoothie? The major ingredient in this smoothie is lentils, which contain more than 25% protein. Furthermore, lentils are high in iron. This mineral is also found in spinach and coconut milk, and the vitamin C found in blueberries may aid your body absorb iron.

Prep Time: 05 min   Cook Time: 00 mins   Servings: 2

Ingredients:

30 g spinach (1 cup)	100 g lentils (1/2 cup)
2.5 cinnamon (1 tsp)	
120 g coconut milk (1/2 cup)	
60 g banana (1/2)	
80 g blueberries (1/2 cup)	

Instructions:

1. Take a blender and then add all the mentioned ingredients in it.
2. Blend all the ingredients till you reach the desired consistency.
3. Serving the smoothie in the serving glass and enjoy.

Nutritional Values:

Calories: 309 g, Fat: 10 g, Carbs: 40 g, Protein: 14.8 g, Iron: 4 mg

Kale & Quinoa Smoothie

This recipe's ingredients are all high in iron content. Quinoa has the same potent plant chemicals as kale, such as kaempferol and quercetin. If you're a vegan or vegetarian, you should eat quinoa frequently because it's a fantastic plant-based source of protein.

Prep Time: 05 min   **Cook Time: 00 mins**   **Servings: 2**

Ingredients:

90 g cooked quinoa (1/2 cup)	
28 cashews (1 oz)	
240 ml coconut milk (1 cup)	
14 g flaxseeds (1 tbsp)	
67 g kale (1 cup)	

Instructions:

1. Take a blender, put all the ingredients in it.
2. Start blending the ingredients till you reach the desired consistency.
3. You can add ice cube or water if you the smoothie consistency to be thin.
4. Pour into glasses and serve.

Nutritional Values:

Calories: 306 g, Fat: 17 g, Carbs: 24 g, Protein: 20 g, Iron: 3.5 mg

Kiwi & Spinach Smoothie

This smoothie is high in iron thanks to the spinach and flaxseeds, and it's high in vitamin C thanks to the lime and kiwis. Meanwhile, the Greek yoghurt adds a creamy texture.

Prep Time: 05 min   **Cook Time: 00 mins**   **Servings: 2**

Ingredients:

120 g greek yogurt (1/2 cup)	30 g spinach (1/2 cup)
200 g kiwis (2)	20 g flaxseed (2 tbsp)
60 g banana (1/2)	
30 g lime (1)	
80 g green apple (1/2)	

Instructions:

1. Firstly, juice the lime.
2. Then add the juice and all the ingredients to the blender.
3. Add ice cubes then blend till you reach smooth consistency.
4. Enjoy.

Nutritional Values:

Calories: 348 g, Fat: 17 g, Carbs: 40 g, Protein: 17 g, Iron: 3.9 mg

Prune Juice Smoothie

Iron is abundant in prune juice, flaxseeds, and spinach. Strawberries and blueberries, on the other hand, are abundant in vitamin C, which may help your body absorb iron better.

Prep Time: 05 min   **Cook Time: 00 mins**   **Servings: 2**

Ingredients:

80 g strawberries (1/2 cup)	
160 g blueberries (1 cup)	
15 g flaxseeds (1 tbsp)	
120 g vanilla greek yogurt (1/2 cup)	
240 ml prune juice (1 cup)	
30 g spinach (1 cup)	

Instructions:

1. Take a blender, put all the ingredients in it.
2. Start mixing till blend well.
3. If you want thin consistency add ice cubes and blend.
4. Serve.

Nutritional Values:

Calories: 284 g, Fat: 3.8 g, Carbs: 53 g, Protein: 9.2 g, Iron: 3.2 mg

Pumkin Overnight Oats

Use any non-dairy milk that you have on hand to make these simple vegan overnight oats. It's a terrific way to use up leftover canned pumpkin, and you can easily double the recipe to prepare healthy breakfasts for the entire week.

Prep Time: 10 min   **Cook Time: 00 mins**   **Servings: 1**

Ingredients:

45 g rolled oats (1/2 cup)	Toasted pecans or pumpkin seeds to garnish
2.5 ml vanilla extract (1/2 tsp)	Salt as per taste
45 g pumpkin puree (3 tbsp)	
10 ml maple syrup (2 tsp)	
80 ml unsweetened almond milk (1/3 cup)	
0.6 g cinnamon (1/4 tsp)	

Instructions:

1. Take a mason jar and add all the ingredients in it.
2. Mix the ingredients then cover the jar with the lid.
3. Refrigerate the jar overnight into the fridge.
4. Serve the oats with toasted pecan or pumpkin seeds on top.

Nutritional Values:

Calories: 218 g, Fat: 4 g, Carbs: 41 g, Protein: 6 g, Iron: 0.3 mg

Overnight Steel Cut Oats

The perfect make-ahead breakfast is overnight steel-cut oats. Make enough for the entire family, or save any leftovers in the fridge to consume throughout the week. These creamy steel-cut oats are delicious with honey, bananas, and raspberries, although any sweetener, chopped fruit, or nut topping will do.

Prep Time: 20 min   Cook Time: 10 mins   Servings: 4

Ingredients:

710 ml unsweetened almond milk (3 cups)	
270 g stee cut oats (1 ½ cups)	
10 ml vanilla extract (2 tsp)	
21 g honey (1 tbsp)	
710 ml water (3 cups)	
1.25 g salt (1/4 tsp)	

Instructions:

1. Take a saucepan and add almond milk, salt, vanilla and water in it.
2. Bring the ingredients to a simmer at moderate temperature.
3. Make sure the mixture is boiling lower the flame and then mix oats into the saucepan.
4. Start cooking the oats for four mins, till they are soft and starts to absorb liquid of the mixture.
5. Let the mixture cool for thirty mins then transfer it to an air-tight container.

6. Keep the container with the lid on into the fridge for twelve hours.
7. After twelve hours take the mixture and again pour it into the saucepan.
8. Boil it at medium heat till the mixture gets thickened.
9. Add honey on top and serve.

Nutritional Values:

Calories: 270 g, Fat: 4 g, Carbs: 86 g, Protein: 8 g, Iron: 0.3 mg

Chocolate Banana Oatmeal

Chocolate Banana Muesli is a delectable and substantial breakfast dish that combines the rich flavours of chocolate, the organic sweetness of bananas, and the sturdy goodness of oats. It's an excellent way to start the day with a filling and nutritious meal.

Prep Time: 05 min   **Cook Time: 10 mins**   **Servings: 1**

Ingredients:

40 g old fashioned rolled oats (1/2 cup)	
235 ml water (1 cup)	
15 g chocolate hazelnut spread (1 tbsp)	
Salt, a pinch	
50 g sliced banana (1/2)	
Flaky sea salt, a pinch	

Instructions:

1. Take a saucepan, put water and salt in it. Warm up till simmering.
2. Mix in oats and cook them cook them for five mins till most of the liquid is absorbed.
3. Turn off the stove and let the oats rest for three mins.
4. Top it with chocolate spread, banana and flaky salt.

Nutritional Values:

Calories: 295 g, Fat: 9 g, Carbs: 50 g, Protein: 7 g, Iron: 3 mg

Lentil and Goat Cheese Toast

The earthy flavours of lentils are combined with the smooth tanginess of goat cheese in this wonderful and gratifying dish. This straightforward but savoury recipe is ideal for a quick and healthful meal.

Prep Time: 10 min　　　**Cook Time: 00 mins**　　**Servings: 2**

Ingredients:

140 g caned French green lentils (2/3 cup)	
30 g goat cheese (2 tbsp)	
Olive sourdough toasted bread, 2 slices	
15 g chopped walnuts (2 tbsp)	

Instructions:

1. Spread 15g of goat cheese on both the slices.
2. Top each toast with walnuts and lentils.

Nutritional Values:

Calories: 282 g, Fat: 11 g, Carbs: 35 g, Protein: 11 g, Iron: 0.3 mg

Breakfast Quesadilla

Recipe for a vegetarian Breakfast Quesadilla with eggs, cheese, spinach, and white beans. Freezer-friendly, healthful, and quick to prepare!

Prep Time: 10 min   Cook Time: 10 mins   Servings: 8

Ingredients:

15 ml milk (1tbsp)	1 g garlic powder (1/2 tsp)
140 g chopped spinach (5 cups)	425 g canned white beans (15 oz.)
2.5 g salt (1/2 tsp)	8 whole wheat tortillas
10 eggs	150 g grated cheese (1 ½ cups)
1 g black pepper (1/2 tsp)	
7.5 ml olive oil (1/2 tbsp)	

Instructions:

1. Whisk the eggs, garlic powder, milk, pepper and salt.
2. Place a nonstick pan at moderate flame and pour olive oil to it.
3. Warm up the oil then put spinach to the pan and heat it up for one min.
4. Mix beans with eggs in the pan and continue cooking till the eggs are scrambled.
5. Season it using salt and pepper.
6. Now to the quesadilla add shredded cheese and egg mixture you have prepared above and then fold the quesadilla in half.

7. Do the same with all the quesadillas and enjoy.

Nutritional Values:

Calories: 373 g, Fat: 16 g, Carbs: 36 g, Protein: 21 g, Iron: 0.4 mg

Avocado Toast

It's high in healthy fats and fiber, creamy, quick to make, and oh so delicious when spread over top of some crunchy toast with a large squeeze of lemon juice!

Prep Time: 10 min   **Cook Time: 40 mins**   **Servings: 4**

Ingredients:

280 g chopped avocados (2)	45 ml lemon juice (3 tbsp)
3 g minced garlic clove (1)	6 g sliced garlic cloves (2)
15 g chopped parsley (1/4 cup)	320 g roma tomatoes (4)
425 g cannellini beans (15 oz)	10 ml balsamic vinegar (2 tsp)
10 g chopped basil leaves (1/4 cup)	15 ml olive oil (1 tbsp)
Pepper & salt, to taste	Pepper & salt, a pinch
15 ml olive oil, 1 tbsp	Gluten free bread, 4 slices
Basil, to garnish	Fleur de sel, to garnish

Instructions:

1. Set the oven temperature at 450 F/220 C.
2. Add the tomatoes in the oil then adjust cut side up on a baking sheet.
3. Insert the mince garlic in the tomato cavities, sprinkle with balsamic vinegar, and apply pepper and salt to taste. To flatten the tomatoes, lightly push them down.
4. Roast for twenty to thirty mins till the tomatoes soften & caramelize. Allow to cool completely before carefully removing and discarding the skin.

5. Meanwhile, blend the parsley, lemon juice, avocados, beans, basil, garlic, salt, & pepper in the food processor till smooth.
6. When tomatoes are done, coat the bread in the leftover oil then toast it on a baking sheet in a hot oven for about five mins or till it is softly golden brown.
7. Arrange the avocado into the four pieces of bread, cover with a toasted tomato slice, and drizzle with fleur de sel and basil leaves.

Nutritional Values:

Calories: 413 g, Fat: 24 g, Carbs: 45 g, Protein: 10 g, Iron: 0.4 mg

Burrito Egg Casserole

A nice breakfast burrito is made up of fluffy eggs as well as a variety of robust fillings. This super-easy casserole combines all of those ingredients into a make-ahead egg meal that's ideal for feeding a crowd.

Prep Time: 10 min   Cook Time: 50 mins   Servings: 6-8

Ingredients:

567 frozen shredded potatoes (20 oz.)	425 g black beans (15 oz)
240 ml sour cream (1 cup)	1 g black pepper (1/4 tsp)
5 g kosher salt (1 tsp)	170 g shredded cheddar cheese (1 ½ cups)
10 eggs	240 ml milk (1 cup)
113 g chopped green chilies (4 oz)	5 g kosher salt, 1 tsp
Cooking spray	

Instructions:

1. Preheat the oven temperature at 375 F, and wire rack at the center.
2. Wrap a baking dish lightly with cooking spray. Combine the shredded potatoes, beans, & chilies in a bowl. Stir everything together, then spread it out evenly.
3. Take a bowl, add eggs, milk, cheese, salt, and pepper. Adjust the veggie mixture on top.

4. Start cooking for forty-five mins, till the exterior is light golden brown. Allow for five mins cooling before slicing. If preferred, top with sliced avocado, cilantro, & salsa.

Nutritional Values:

Calories: 389 g, Fat: 22 g, Carbs: 26 g, Protein: 19 g, Iron: 3.9 mg

Breakfast Sandwich

The Breakfast Sandwich is a tasty and filling dish that blends the flavours of a traditional Mexican breakfast with the ease of a portable sandwich. It's the ideal way to start the day with a rush of robust and hearty flavours.

Prep Time: 05 min   **Cook Time: 10 mins**   **Servings: 1**

Ingredients:

15g salsa ranchera (1tbsp)	30 g refried beans (2 tbsp)
100 g English muffin (1)	
30 g guacamole (2 tbsp)	
Pepper & salt, taste	
30 g guacamole (2 tbsp)	
1 egg	

Instructions:

1. Fry the egg and then season it using pepper & salt.
2. Take English muffin and on one side of it pour beans and guacamole then top it with salsa.
3. Place the other half of the bun and enjoy.

Nutritional Values:

Calories: 250 g, Fat: 7 g, Carbs: 32 g, Protein: 12.7 g, Iron: 0.3 mg

Steaks with goulash sauce and sweet potato fries

Fuel your appetite with an irresistible meal that incorporated the goodness of iron-rich cuts of beef, powerful goulash sauce and highly nutritious potato fries. A delectable recipe to conquer anemia.

Prep Time: 10 min　　　　**Cook Time: 25 mins**　　　**Servings: 2**

Ingredients:

14 g thyme leaves (1 tbsp)	250 g sweet potatoes (11/8 cup)
2 garlic cloves	1 tsp vegetable bouillon powder
14 g tomato purée (1 tbsp)	85 g cherry tomatoes (1/4 cup plus 4 tsp)
200 g bag baby spinach (2 cups)	2 small onions
15 ml rapeseed oil (3 tsp)	5 g smoked paprika (1 tsp)
1 green pepper	

Instructions:

1. Set the oven temperature to 240C.
2. Take a bowl, add thyme, potatoes with oil in it, then distribute them and set aside over the rack till cooked.
3. Take a pan and warm oil in it. Add the onions and cook for five mins.
4. Cover it with the lid and mix well till they become charred.
5. Mix in the garlic & pepper (green), close the pan with lid & start cooking for five mins, then add the potatoes and start baking for fifteen mins.

6. Add the peppers and paprika into the onions, pour some water in the pan and whisk in the tomato puree, bouillon and cherry tomatoes. Close the lid and cook more for ten mins.
7. Heat the steak for two to three mins from every side then rest for five mins.
8. Apply the goulash sauce onto the plates and top of beef using spoon.
9. Serve with chips and spinach together.

Nutritional Values:

Calories: 452 g, Fat: 14 g, Carbs: 43 g, Protein: 33 g, Iron: 4.2 mg

Mini lamb roasts with balsamic vegetables

Do you want to say goodbye to anemia? Then your wait is over. It is a mouthwatering feast that delights both your culinary buds and body needs. Learn to adore a nutritional and anemia friendly lunch which improves your health as well as gives you the best culinary pleasure.

Prep Time: 25 min   **Cook Time: 25 mins**   **Servings: 4**

Ingredients:

14 ml olive oil (1 tbsp)	small mint leaves, for sprinkling
2 medium zucchinis	1 medium red onion
80 ml balsamic vinegar (1/3 cup)	8 dutch (baby) carrots
2 mini lamb roasts	
14 g rosemary leaves (1 tbsp)	
1 red capsicum	

Instructions:

1. Set the oven temperature to 200C.
2. Take a pan, add lamb in it, then put rosemary while drizzling it with oil.
3. Take another pan, put onion, carrot, vinegar, zucchini, oil and capsicum.
4. Mix them all to combine well. Grill lamb and vegetables for twenty-five mins till they cooked.
5. Drizzle lamb and vegetables with pepper and salt.
6. Set the lamb aside for five mins while it is covered.
7. Serve vegetables and lamb with mint leaves on top.

Nutritional Values:

Calories: 405 g, Fat: 22.1 g, Carbs: 19.9 g, Protein: 32.6 g, Iron: 4 mg

Beef Teriyaki Skewers

Boost your energy and unleash the power of iron with beef teriyaki skewers. It enhances your iron level to fight against anemia. You are going to taste the perfect combination of mouthwatering spices and nourishing benefits with every savoury morsel.

Prep Time: 15 min   Cook Time: 10 mins   Servings: 4

Ingredients:

240 ml soy sauce (1 cup)	300 g brown sugar (1 ½ cups)
¼ inch slices bamboo skewers, soaked in water	60 ml vegetable oil (¼ cup)
120 ml water (½ cup)	
4 lb. boneless round steak (65 oz.)	
120 ml pineapple juice, optional (½ cup)	
3 garlic cloves	

Instructions:

1. Take a large bowl, add garlic, pineapple juice, water, brown sugar, soy sauce, and vegetable oil. Mix them together.
2. Add beef slices into the mixture & stir to marinade.
3. Wrap the bowl with plastic. Place marinated beef in refrigerator for twenty-four hours.
4. Remove beef from the fridge, taking effort to shake off and eliminate any extra liquid.
5. Place the beef slices in a zig-zag way onto the skewers.

6. Lightly oil the grate and set the grill to moderate heat.
7. Cook the skewers for three mins per side till beef is cooked well.

Nutritional Values:

Calories: 274 g, Fat: 8 g, Carbs: 9 g, Protein: 37 g, Iron: 3 mg

Vegan Lentil Stew

The versatile feast is perfect for lunch, embark on a savoury journey with our vegan lentil stew. Relish every wonderful, plant-powered morsel and feed your body with iron. For those embracing a vegan lifestyle and looking the ways to boost their iron levels, this amazing stew will provide you a delightful substitute.

Prep Time: 15 min   Cook Time: 45 mins   Servings: 6

Ingredients:

14 ml olive oil (1 tbsp)	48 oz vegetable broth (6 cups)
3 cloves garlic	½ tsp dried thyme (2.5 g)
5 ml Italian seasoning (1 tsp)	1 onion
400 g diced tomatoes (14 oz)	1.25 g cayenne pepper (1/4 tsp)
2 medium carrots	14 g tomato paste, optional (1 tbsp)
2.5 g cumin (½ tsp)	360 g dried lentils (1 ½ cups)
2 stalks celery	salt, to taste
2.5 g ground paprika (½ tsp)	1 bay leaf
1 potato	

Instructions:

1. Take a pan, warm water or oil at medium temperature.
2. Add onions and garlic in it and start cooking for about three to four mins.

3. Add paprika, thyme, Italian seasoning, cumin, celery, lentils, carrots, tomato paste, tomatoes, vegetable broth, bay leaf and potatoes and simmer for thirty seconds.
4. Start heating for about forty mins till stew has desired flavour or it comes to boil, turn down the flame.
5. Take off bay leaf from the heat, drizzle with pepper and salt then serve.

Nutritional Values:

Calories: 292 g, Fat: 5 g, Carbs: 43 g, Protein: 19 g, Iron: 4.8 mg

Mussels with chorizo, beans & cavolo nero

Looking for anemia friendly diet? Try this captivating dish and dive into the ocean of iron-rich delight. The tempting combo of sturdy beans, chorizo and high in iron cavolo nero welcomes every succulent mussel. The recipe is carefully developed to give a substantial amount of iron and to please your taste buds.

Prep Time: 15 min   Cook Time: 10 mins   Servings: 2

Ingredients:

2 garlic cloves	2 chopped shallots
14 ml olive oil (1 tbsp)	100 g cooking chorizo (3.5 oz)
100 g cavolo nero, stems removed, leaves shredded (1 cup)	150 ml white wine (1 ¼ cup)
1 lemon	500 g mussels (18 oz)
Chopped bunch parsley, separated leaves & stalks	
400 g can cannellini beans (14 oz)	

Instructions:

1. Take a pan, cook slowly the chorizo, shallots, stalks, parsley and garlic in the oil, with the lid for about five mins, till the shallots are softened.
2. Put the cavolo nero and cook for more mins then add the wine and simmer for further one min.
3. After adding the beans then making sure that the mussels are thoroughly coated in sauce, cover the pot with the lid.

4. Simmer for a few mins, shake the pan to let out the mussel juices, till they have all opened.
5. Sprinkle the parsley and pour some lemon juice over them the serve.

Nutritional Values:

Calories: 596 g, Fat: 26 g, Carbs: 24 g, Protein: 49 g, Iron: 4 mg

Lamb & squash biryani with cucumber raita

Prepare for a fantastic trip of taste and vigour. Experience a gastronomic journey with this delicious lunch recipe as it nourishes your body and awakens your appetite. Refreshing cucumber raita gives a cooling touch.

Prep Time: 10 min   Cook Time: 25 mins   Servings: 4

Ingredients:

40 g chopped ginger (8 tsp)	400 g lean lamb steaks (14 oz)
4 onions	15 g ground coriander (3 tsp)
170 g basmati rice (1 ¼ cup)	2 chopped red chilies
10 g cumin seeds (2 tsp)	320 g diced butternut squash (1 ½ cup)
1 cucumber	Chopped handful coriander
60 g chopped mint (4 tbsp)	10 g vegetable bouillon powder (2 tsp)
100 ml bio yogurt (1/2 cup)	2 garlic cloves
20 ml rapeseed oil (4 tsp)	

Instructions:

1. Add the lamb with the garlic, ground coriander and chopped ginger then set aside.
2. Warm oil in a pan. Stir-fry the remaining ginger, onions, and chili at high heat, till they began to soften.
3. Heat for a few mins, put the squash in and cook rice.

4. Further add all the additional spices then mix the bouillon and hot water.
5. Cover it with the lid and cook for twenty mins.
6. Take a bowl, combine yogurt, cucumber & mint together to make raita.
7. Chill half of it for later. Warm the leftover oil, mix lamb steaks and start cooking about five mins or till it is browned and tendered, while the rice is ready.
8. Add the spiced rice with the coriander.
9. Serve with topped coriander leaves and raita.

Nutritional Values:

Calories: 463 g, Fat: 15 g, Carbs: 49 g, Protein: 30 g, Iron: 3 mg

Oysters with chili & ginger dressing

In every bite, enjoy the flavour of the ocean while gaining more nutrients. Indulge in a treat that feeds your body and touches your taste senses. The salty jewels are served with a zingy, energetic dressing made with ingredients high in iron.

Prep Time: 15 min   **Cook Time: 00 mins**   **Servings: 4**

Ingredients:

12 shucked oysters	1 garlic clove
For the sauce:	4 sliced onions
Thumb-sized piece ginger	28 ml mirin (2 tbsp)
28 ml sesame oil (2 tbsp)	1 red chili
Chopped bunch chives, optional	
14 ml soy sauce (1 tbsp)	

Instructions:

1. Shuck your oysters, if they are not prepared before.
2. Take a bowl, add all of the ingredients and mix them together to make the sauce.
3. Pour the sauce over the oysters top with chopped chives and serve immediately.

Nutritional Values:

Calories: 90 g, Fat: 6 g, Carbs: 6 g, Protein: 4 g, Iron: 6 mg

Lentil & Beetroot Salad with Steak

Enjoy a flavourful lunch that supports your health quest while feeding your body and satisfying your appetites. A wholesome salad made out of delicious sirloin, colourful beetroots, and nutrient-dense lentils. It also helps to increase the iron consumption.

Prep Time: 20 min Cook Time: 05 mins Servings: 4

Ingredients:

30 ml light sour cream (2 tbsp)	250 g whole baby beetroot (2 cups)
3 parsley leaves	400 g fillet steak (14 oz)
5 g honey, optional (1 tsp)	30 ml horseradish cream (2 tbsp)
150 g kale leaf & spinach mix (2 cups)	400g can lentils (14 oz)
5 ml olive oil spray (1 tsp)	2 onions
2 peeled oranges	1 lemon, juiced and zest

Instructions:

1. Take a pan, warm the oil in it then put steak in it.
2. Start cooking for three to five mins or till cooked to your preferences while keep rotating.
3. Transfer in the serving dish, loosely wrap it with foil and set aside for five mins. Then make thin slices of it.
4. In the meantime, take a bowl, add sour cream, honey, horseradish cream and lemon together to make the dressing then season respectively.
5. Take another bowl, add salad mix and dressing together in it.

6. Properly arrange orange slices, steak, beetroot, parsley, onion & lentils on plates then serve.

Nutritional Values:

Calories: 382 g, Fat: 15.3 g, Carbs: 28.8 g, Protein: 30 g, Iron: 7.4 mg

Chickpea, spinach and egg curry

Salutations to curry lovers. Explore a satisfying curry that nourishes your quest for health while satisfying your cravings. Enjoy the vivid flavours of our anemia-friendly chickpea, spinach, and egg curry.

Prep Time: 25 min   Cook Time: 30 mins   Servings: 2

Ingredients:

14 ml olive oil (1 tbsp)	5 g garlic granules (1 tsp)
400 g tin chopped tomatoes (1.8 cup)	2 eggs
5 g black mustard seeds (1 tsp)	400 g tin chickpeas (14 oz)
14 ml lemon juice (1 tbsp)	10 g curry powder (2 tsp)
180 g baby leaf spinach (6 oz)	30 g cumin seeds (2 tbsp)
30 g chopped coriander for garnish (2 tbsp)	100 ml boiling water (3½ oz)
Ground pepper & salt	5 g ground ginger (1 tsp)

Instructions:

1. Take a pan, warm up the water till simmering. Cook the eggs in it for eight to ten mins or till they are cooked properly.
2. Set aside to cool or when it is ready to handle, shell, halve and safe. At the same time, take a frying pan and warm the oil in it.
3. Add the curry powder, ground ginger, black mustard seeds, garlic granules & cumin then stir-fry it for a min.

4. Sprinkle with pepper and salt and stir-fry chickpeas, tomatoes and lemon juice in the boiling water.
5. Cook it for six to eight mins, while keep stirring till get thickened.
6. Then add the spinach and cook, till it wilts.
7. Adjust the curry between two small bowls.
8. Add some curry powder and two egg halves on the top of each bowls.
9. Sprinkle with coriander and serve right away.

Nutritional Values:

Calories: 441 g, Fat: 20 g, Carbs: 92 g, Protein: 26 g, Iron: 2 mg

The Ultimate Lamb Burger

Get ready for a unique, bold, and satisfying burger experience. A scrumptious burger that satisfies your tastes and promotes your health is made with a juicy lamb patty that is brimming with herbs, spices, and iron-rich toppings. It relishes the greatest flavour journey.

Prep Time: 10 min   Cook Time: 10 mins   Servings: 4

Ingredients:

15 ml olive oil (1 tbsp)	Mint sprigs for sprinkle
4 brioche burger buns	15 ml red wine vinegar (1 tbsp)
1 baby cos lettuce	100 g tzatziki (⅓ cup)
8 slices canned beetroot	2 tomatoes
600 g lean lamb mince (20 oz.)	1 red onion small
4 cheese slices	

Instructions:

1. Take a big bowl, add the lamb mince, toss with pepper & salt.
2. From four patties, using hands. Heat up a frying pan or Barbecue to moderate high flame.
3. Apply oil on both sides of the patties. Cook for two to three mins, till the patties are lightly browned at the bottom.
4. Put the cheese on top after rotating the patties.
5. After cheese has melted, cook for another two mins, till bottoms are lightly browned.
6. Place patties on a plate covered with foil.

7. Take a bowl, add vinegar & onion. Sprinkle with salt and toss then marinate.
8. Add some tzatziki on the bottom halves of the buns.
9. Add lamb patties, beetroot, baby cos, pickled onion and tomatoes on the top.
10. Garnish with mint sprigs and serve straight away.

Nutritional Values:

Calories: 439 g, Fat: 26 g, Carbs: 26 g, Protein: 24 g, Iron: 3 mg

Mushroom & Tofu Stir-Fry

Want to enjoy a wholesome and delicious meal. Try our anemia-friendly mushroom and tofu stir-fry to enhance your iron consumption. It is the perfect moment to go on a culinary adventure of wellness and desires of hunger.

Prep Time: min Cook Time: mins Servings:

Ingredients:

1 lb mixed mushrooms (5 cups)	1 container baked tofu (8 oz)
1 bunch scallions	15 g ginger (1 tbsp)
1 clove garlic	
45 ml oyster sauce (3 tbsp)	
60 ml canola oil (4 tbsp)	
1 red bell pepper	

Instructions:

1. Take a skillet, warm oil at higher flame.
2. Add the bell pepper and mushrooms, simmer for about four mins, stir constantly till tendered.
3. Add the ginger, scallions & garlic, and cook for an additional thirty seconds.
4. Put the vegetables in bowl. Mix the tofu and the extra oil in pan.
5. Start cooking for three to four mins, till becomes golden.
6. Mix well the Oyster sauce and the vegetables. Cook them for about one min while stirring.

Nutritional Values:

Calories: 171 g, Fat: 13 g, Carbs: 9 g, Protein: 8 g, Iron: 2 mg

Sauteed Balsamic Spinach

Enjoy a flavour explosion that will energize you. This colourful side dish is made up of ideal sautéed, delicate spinach, tangy balsamic sauce, and vegetables that are high in iron. It helps to boost your iron levels in the body.

Prep Time: 05 min   Cook Time: 10 mins   Servings: 4

Ingredients:

3 cloves garlic	
30 ml balsamic glaze (2 tbsp)	
1 lb fresh baby spinach (16 oz)	
Grated pecorino romano cheese, optional	
30 ml olive oil (2 tbsp)	

Instructions:

1. Clean the spinach using a salad spinner. Then place it aside.
2. Take an oven or a pot, warm the olive oil at moderate flame.
3. Thinly slice the garlic and then mix it to the sauce pan using knife.
4. Put the spinach after cooking for thirty seconds, till the flavour starts to come out.
5. Before adding the balsamic glaze, pressing it down till the spinach wilted.
6. Transfer it to a serving bowl and combine well.
7. Then garnish it with cheese and serve warmly.

Nutritional Values:

Calories: 104 g, Fat: 7 g, Carbs: 8 g, Protein: 3 g, Iron: 3 mg

Creamy Mushroom Steak

The perfect lunch meal for those who are fighting with anemia disease and want to nourish their bodies with the components high in iron, creamy mushroom steak is the ideal lunch as it refills your iron deficiency.

Prep Time: 15 min   Cook Time: 20 mins   Servings: 3

Ingredients:

60 g salted butter (¼ cup)	5 g garlic (1 tbsp)
10 g organic garlic powder (2 tsp)	480 ml heavy whipping cream (2 cups)
7.5 g salt (1 ½ tsp)	14 g black pepper (1 tbsp)
240 g sliced baby bella mushrooms (8 oz)	Garlic cloves & rosemary stems
Ground black pepper and salt to marinate the meat	14 g olive oil (1 Tbsp)
1 pack of angus N.Y strip steak	

Instructions:

1. Use grounded black pepper and salt to marinate the steak.
2. Add butter in the heated skillet, further cook herbs and steak by adding them in it or till they are cooked halfway.
3. Wrap them using foil and place it aside.
4. Pour oil in the heated pan and cook garlic for thirty seconds. Further add mushrooms and cook them till mushrooms are tendered.

5. Add whipping cream, salt, garlic powder and black pepper in it and start cooking to make the thickened sauce.
6. Further mix them with steak and cook them on moderate temperature till well.
7. Take out from the flame and drizzle with herbs and serve right away with baked potato wedges.

Nutritional Values:

Calories: 804 g, Fat: 56.5 g, Carbs: 7.1 g, Protein: 70.6 g, Iron: 5.4 mg

Penne with Eggplant, Tomatoes & Chick peas

Embrace a delightful road to wellness. Increase your consumption of iron with our anemia-friendly penne with eggplant, tomatoes and chickpeas. This vibrant pasta dish is a flavourful and nourishing meal that satisfies your cravings and nourishes your health.

Prep Time: 10 min   Cook Time: 10 mins   Servings: 4

Ingredients:

60 ml olive oil (1/4 cup)	1 large eggplant
1 large sweet onion	Kosher salt
1 can chick peas	3 oz crumbled ricotta salata (1 cup)
Ground black pepper	30 g minced garlic (2 tbsp)
Basil leaves for garnish	1 can chopped tomatoes
300 g penne pasta (10 oz)	

Instructions:

1. Take a pot, pour a salted water to a boil. Start cooking the penne till nearly done as per mentioned on the pack.
2. Take out half cup from the penne water.
3. Use a skillet, warm the oil at moderate flame till bubbling.
4. Put the eggplant and simmer for five to six mins, stirring periodically, till it starts to soften.
5. Lower the flame to normal, put the onions & starts cooking for about six mins, while stirring continuously.
6. Stirring constantly till they start to soften. Put the garlic and simmer for about thirty secs, till slightly aromatic.

7. Add the tomatoes, chickpeas, ¼ cup of the pasta water, ½ tsp pepper and 1 tsp of salt. Cook for about two mins, till the mixture is just heated well.
8. Toss sauce mixture and pasta in the saucepan after adding it. If the resulting mixture is too thick, then add the extra ½ cup of the pasta water.
9. Seasoning as to taste. In a serving bowl, separating the penne mixture.
10. Serve the penne dish and sprinkle with basil and crumbled ricotta salata.

Nutritional Values:

Calories: 455 g, Fat: 12 g, Carbs: 65 g, Protein: 18 g, Iron: 4.5 mg

Sheet Pan Steak and Veggies

It's time to savour the goodness. A mouthwatering and satisfying supper which helps to make you fit and your goals is created on a single skillet using a juicy steak, vibrant roasted veggies, and iron-rich foods. It will refuel your iron stores while providing a delectable meal.

Prep Time: 15 min　　　**Cook Time: 15 mins**　　　**Servings: 6**

Ingredients:

30 g olive oil (2 tbsp)	5 g dried thyme (1 tsp)
Ground black pepper and kosher salt to taste	
2 lb baby red potatoes (30 oz)	
3 minced cloves garlic	
455 g broccoli florets (16 oz)	
2 lb sirloin steak (30 oz)	

Instructions:

1. Set the oven temperature to broil. Lightly spray the baking tray.
2. Take a pot, add salted water in it and cook potatoes till simmered for twelve to fifteen mins.
3. In the single layer on the baking sheet, adjust broccoli and potatoes that has been prepared.
4. Add thyme, olive oil, garlic, pepper and salt in it. Combine with a gentle toss.
5. Add steaks on a baking sheet and sprinkle with pepper and salt as required to taste.

6. Put into oven and broil for about four to five mins each side or till the steak is browned and burned at the corners.
7. Serve straight away and sprinkle with garlic butter.

Nutritional Values:

Calories: 230 g, Fat: 8 g, Carbs: 9 g, Protein: 30 g, Iron: 2.5 mg

Kale Quinoa Salad – With Lemon Dressing

Every bite will bring you fresh flavours and renewed vigour. The combination of nutrient-dense kale, protein-rich quinoa, and a tangy lemon dressing results in a light and filling salad that feeds your body and tickles the appetite receptors.

Prep Time: 05 min   Cook Time: 10 mins   Servings: 6

Ingredients:

240 g canned chickpeas (1 cup)	420 g of chopped kale (6 cups)
5 g olive oil (1 tsp)	60 g diced red onion (1/3 cup)
60 g diced cucumber (1/3 cup)	10 g chopped dill (1/8 cup)
Kale salad dressing	60 g pepitas (1/3 cup)
240 g cooked quinoa (1 cup)	10 g ped parsley (1/8 cup)
60 g golden raisins (1/3 cup)	60 g crumbled feta cheese (1/3 cup)

Instructions:

1. To prepare the kale, give it an extensive rinse under cold water, then put it onto a clean towel and dry it well.
2. After that, chop the kale using knife and add it to the bowl.
3. Season it with a little salt and pour some olive oil over it.
4. For one to two mins, rub and press the kale to your hands to make it soft.
5. After that, wait for then mins before tossing the salad respectively.
6. To the bowl containing kale, add the leftover salad components in the absence of the dressing.

7. Pout the kale salad dressing over the salad after mixing it. Serve after mixing everything together.

Nutritional Values:

Calories: 400 g, Fat: 13.5 g, Carbs: 25.2 g, Protein: 6.1 g, Iron: 2 mg

Lentil soup with goat's cheese toast

Say good-bye to anemia, one teaspoon at a time. A rich and nourishing soup that delights your desire for flavour and gives you an enjoyable iron boost originates from velvety lentils, savoury spices, and a zesty goat's cheese toast.

Prep Time: 25 min   Cook Time: 3hrs Servings: 4

Ingredients:

2 celery sticks	115g red lentils (1/2 cup)
1 chopped swede	1 chopped onion
1 baguette	2 cans diced tomatoes
500ml massel vegetable liquid stock (2 cups)	100g goat's cheese (1/2 cup)
1 chopped carrot	1 garlic clove
10 g chopped chives (2 tsp)	15 g ground cumin (3 tsp)

Instructions:

1. Use a slow cooker, add garlic, celery, lentils, swede, stock, onion, cumin, and tomato in it.
2. Cover the mixture and start cooking for three hours, till soup is thickened and vegetables are softened.
3. Set the grill to higher temperature. Put the bread on a baking tray. Start baking till browned on each side for two mins.
4. Take a bowl, mix chives and goat's cheese together. Toast with cheese on it.
5. Serve the soup in dishes, topped with goat's cheese. Enjoy!

Nutritional Values:

Calories: 282 g, Fat: 11 g, Carbs: 35 g, Protein: 11 g, Iron: 6.1 mg

Pan-Seared Steak with Crispy Herbs & Escarole

A symphony of flavours is created when succulent steak, a crunchy herb crust, and vivid escarole come together to fulfil desires while nourishing the body. Enjoy a steak experience that will make better your health and palate.

Prep Time: 10 min   Cook Time: 20 mins   Servings: 4

Ingredients:

2.5 g salt (1/2 tsp)	28 ml olive oil (2 tbsp)
4 garlic cloves	1 sprig rosemary
3 sprigs sage	450 g sirloin steak (16 oz)
450 g chopped escarole (16 oz)	
2.5 g black pepper (1/2 tsp)	
5 sprigs Thyme	

Instructions:

1. Add pepper and salt to the steak.
2. Warm the skillet at higher temperature. Put the steak and cook for about three mins, till browned on one side.
3. Add garlic, sage, oil, rosemary and thyme in the meat. Cook the herbs while stirring continuously.
4. Place the steak to a platter and garnish with garlic and herbs. Wrap foil in a tent.
5. Add escarole and remaining one fourth tsp of pepper and salt in the heated pan.
6. Cook for about two mins, till escarole begins to wilt, while stirring.

7. Thinly slice the steak. Serve with the crispy herbs and escarole.

Nutritional Values:

Calories: 244 g, Fat: 12 g, Carbs: 10 g, Protein: 26 g, Iron: 4 mg

Vegan Chickpea Tuna Salad

Looking for anemia friendly diet? Try this captivating dish and dive into the vibrancy. This plant-based pleasure provides a filling option that fulfils cravings and encourages a healthy, anemia-friendly diet. It is loaded with protein-rich chickpeas, ocean-inspired flavours, and iron-rich components.

Prep Time: 15 min   Cook Time: 00 mins   Servings: 4

Ingredients:

115 g diced yellow onion (½ cup)	14 g pickle relish (1 tbsp)
15 g parsley (1 tbsp)	2 g kosher salt (¼ tsp)
0.5 g black pepper (1/8 tsp)	Bread slices, or lettuce, or crackers, optional
1 can chickpeas	10 g diced celery (¼ cup)
10 g vegan mayonnaise (2 tsp)	
2.5 g dried dill (½ tsp)	

Instructions:

1. Take a bowl, combine all the ingredients in it.
2. Smash chickpeas with a fork or potato masher.
3. Put the extra ingredients and mix well.
4. Serve with toast, bread or lettuce.

Nutritional Values:

Calories: 176 g, Fat: 9 g, Carbs: 21 g, Protein: 5 g, Iron: 1 mg

Skillet Moussaka

Nourish your body while pleasing your palate. This hearty anemia friendly recipe offers a vulnerable alternative for anyone looking for a healthy and delicious supper while supporting their health journey as it is packed with components rich in iron and layers of wholesome taste.

Prep Time: 10 min   Cook Time: 28 mins   Servings: 6

Ingredients:

7.5 g oregano leaves (1½ tsp)	2 eggs
1 large eggplant	7.5 g whole thyme leaves (1½ tsp)
2.5 g organic mint (1/2 tsp)	1 can tomato sauce
1 jar alfredo sauce	60 g flour (½ cup)
1 lb lean ground beef (16 oz)	
2.5 g salt (½ tsp)	

Instructions:

1. Warm the skillet at normal temperature.
2. Put one tsp of each of the oregano, salt, thyme, ground beef and mint.
3. Start cooking them and toss till the beef gives brown colour.
4. Add eggplant and cook for about three to five mins and mix till it begins too soft.
5. Take a bowl, add thyme, flour, half tsp of each of the oregano, alfredo sauce and egg and mix well.
6. Drizzle on the meat mixture.

7. Cook for about ten to fifteen mins under cover or till alfredo custard is thickened and set well.

Nutritional Values:

Calories: 296 g, Fat: 16 g, Carbs: 18 g, Protein: 20 g, Iron: 3 mg

Gochujang-Roasted Potatoes

Prepare to be surprised with a fresh take on an old favourite. Take your potato game to the next level with Gochujang-Roasted Potatoes. These crispy golden potato nuggets are lavishly coated in a spicy and savoury gochujang glaze, resulting in a flavour explosion that will get your taste buds dancing.

Prep Time: 15 min   **Cook Time: 30 mins**   **Servings: 4**

Ingredients:

15 g gochujang (2 tbsp)	10 g soy sauce (2 tsp)
1 pinch red pepper flakes, optional	½ medium lime
18 ml grapeseed oil (2 ½ tbsp)	5 g sesame oil (1 tsp)
2 russet chunk potatoes	
5 g salt (1 tsp)	
2 scallions	

Instructions:

1. Take a bowl and add potatoes in it (To eliminate extra starch, rinse potatoes in a colander; Drain well).
2. Further add one Tbsp of salt and oil then combine them to marinate.
3. Start baking them in oven for almost four mins at higher temperature. Cover the potatoes and cook again for two mins or till potatoes are easily cut using fork. To drain, move to a coriander.
4. Set the oven temperature to 400 F/ 200 C. Cover the baking sheet using parchment paper.

5. Take the bowl used to fry the potatoes, combine the red pepper flakes, one and a half tbsp of oil, sesame oil and soy sauce.
6. Spread the potatoes out, after returning them to the bowl and coating them.
7. Roast potatoes in the heated oven for about twenty mins, flipping once or two times, till it brown.
8. Take out from the oven and drizzle scallions. Add lime juice on top.

Nutritional Values:

Calories: 192 g, Fat: 10 g, Carbs: 25 g, Protein: 3 g, Iron: 1 mg

White Bean Soup

Prep Time: 10 min   **Cook Time: 15 mins**   **Servings: 4**

Ingredients:

30 g olive oil (2 tbsp)	4 chopped garlic cloves
30 oz. chicken stock (4 cups)	340 g baby spinach (12 oz)
400 g cannelini beans pureed (14 oz)	Pepper and salt to taste
Chopped parsley	400 g cannellini beans drained (14 oz)
Grated parmesan cheese	
250 g ditalini pasta (8 oz)	

Instructions:

1. Take a pot, warm water in it and cook the pasta as well as cook the soup.
2. Take another pot, warm the oil and lightly brown the garlic in it.
3. Add the cannellini beans, chicken stock, herbs and pureed beans when you notice, it begins to brown.
4. Sprinkle with pepper and salt in it and turn up the flame and start simmer.
5. Then lower down the heat and cook for ten mins.
6. Cook frozen spinach in the oven then squeeze out the extra liquid.
7. Put the spinach and cook till it wilts.
8. Immediately serve with pasta and top with parmesan cheese.

Nutritional Values:

Calories: 265 g, Fat: 6 g, Carbs: 35 g, Protein: 16 g, Iron: 4.5 mg

Garlic & Herb Steak Pizza

Looking for anemia friendly diet? Try this captivating dish and dig your teeth with garlic & herb steak pizza is a flavourful pleasure. Succulent beef, aromatic garlic, and fragrant herbs combine atop a crispy crust to develop a tantalizing blend of flavours that whisks your taste senses away on a gourmet pizza trip.

Prep Time: 15 min   Cook Time: 15 mins   Servings: 6

Ingredients:

260 g shredded part-skim mozzarella cheese (1 ½ cups)	4 g pepper (¾ tsp)
1 prebaked thin pizza crust	120 g garlic-herb spreadable cheese (½ cup)
480 g chopped spinach (2 cups)	14 g olive oil (1 tbsp)
¾ tsp salt (4 g)	240 g sliced mushrooms (1 cup)
1 lb beef top sirloin steak (16 oz)	
240 g sliced red onion (1 cup)	

Instructions:

1. Heat the oven to 450 F.
2. Sprinkle pepper and salt to the steak.
3. Warm oil in a big skillet, at medium heat.
4. Steak is added. If thermometer reads 145 degrees for a medium rare completion, cook five to six min on every side. Tale out of pan.
5. In the meantime, pour garlic-herb cheese over the pizza crust placed on a baking sheet that has not been oiled.

6. Add onion and spinach for sprinkle. Slice the steak and place it on the pizza.
7. Till the cheese is melted, bake for about ten mins.
8. Divide twelve pieces into cut.

Nutritional Values:

Calories: 440 g, Fat: 23 g, Carbs: 29 g, Protein: 30 g, Iron: 6 mg

Mediterranean Pork and Orzo

Are you a seafood enthusiast? Then you have delicious Pork and Orzo lunch dish is going to take you on an eating adventure through the Mediterranean. A delightful dish that meets you up and explore your taste buds to the Mediterranean's sunny coasts is made with delicious pork, substantial orzo, and a blend of Mediterranean spices.

Prep Time: 10 min   Cook Time: 20 mins   Servings: 6

Ingredients:

30 g olive oil (2 tbsp)	240 g grape tomatoes (1 cup)
250 g uncooked orzo pasta (1 1/4 cups)	5 g coarse ground black pepper (1 tsp)
1 pkg Baby Spinach	3 quarts water
170 g crumbled feta cheese (¾ cup)	
2 pork tenderloin	
2.5 g salt (1/4 tsp)	

Instructions:

1. Pepper the pork, cut into 1-inch pieces.
2. At medium heat cook pork in oil for about eight to ten mins in a big skillet, till no pinker.
3. In the meantime, put water to a simmer in the pan.
4. Add the orzo and salt then boil for eight mins, without the lid.
5. Add spinach, till orzo is cooked and spinach has wilted, cook for about additional forty-five to sixty secs.

6. Cook and toss the pork with the tomatoes for a min till cooked completely.
7. Drain orzo mixture, combine with feta cheese and the pork combination.

Nutritional Values:

Calories: 231.8 g, Fat: 9.2 g, Carbs: 29.3 g, Protein: 8.3 g, Iron: 2.5 mg

Grilled Garlic Butter Shrimp

Grilled Garlic Butter Shrimp is a delectable recipe that highlights the natural flavours of shrimp while also incorporating the rich and savoury flavour of garlic butter. It's a delectable and straightforward recipe that brings out the most in delicious grilled prawns.

Prep Time: 15 min   Cook Time: 15 mins   Servings: 4

Ingredients:

1 minced shallot	Kosher salt & ground black pepper
2.5 g crushed red pepper flakes (¼ tsp)	2 lemons
1 ½ lb medium shrimp (24 oz)	
10 g chopped parsley leaves (2 tbsp)	
120 g unsalted butter (½ cup)	
4 cloves garlic	

Instructions:

1. At a medium flame, melt the butter in a small skillet.
2. Mix red pepper flakes, shallot and garlic till aromatic for about two mins.
3. Pepper and salt are then added to taste, add pepper and salt to taste after threading the prawns onto the skewers.
4. Use two Tbsp of butter mixture to the brush. Heat the grill at moderate high temperature.
5. Grill the skewers and start cooking for about three to four mins, till the prawns are pink and translucent, rotating periodically.
6. Add lemons, cut side down, during the last two mins of grilling.

7. Serve straight away. Sprinkle with the remaining butter combination. If like, drizzle with parsley and lemons.

Nutritional Values:

Calories: 224 g, Fat: 10 g, Carbs: 1.3 g, Protein: 32 g, Iron: 1 mg

Greek Pasta

Be set to relish an outstanding blend of flavour and nutrition that will have your taste buds clamouring for more. Taste prevails with our Greek pasta. This iron rich dish interacts cooked pasta with enticing Greek flavours and an infusion of iron-rich superfoods.

Prep Time: 20 min   Cook Time: 30 mins   Servings: 8

Ingredients:

2 lb cooked chicken breast (4 cups)	1 can tomato sauce
5 g dried basil (1 tsp)	60 g chopped red onion (1/4 cup)
480 ml canola oil (2 cups)	1 package chopped spinach
1 pkg whole wheat penne pasta	5 g dried oregano (1 tsp)
30 g chopped green pepper (2 tbsp)	1 can diced tomatoes
120 g crumbled feta cheese (1/2 cup)	120 g shredded part-skim mozzarella cheese (1/2 cup)

Instructions:

1. Drain pasta after cooking according to the instructions on the package.
2. Add the chicken, spinach, green pepper, tomato, oregano, tomato sauce, onion, pasta, olives and basil in a big bowl.
3. Place in the sprayed baking dish.
4. Apply cheese at the top. Start baking for about twenty-five to thirty mins, at 400 F/200 C, uncovered, till cheese is melted and cooked completely.
5. Cold casserole and frozen, under cover. Freeze slightly in fridge at night, to use.

6. Before baking, take out of fridge thirty mins. Heat the oven to 400 F.
7. As recommended, baked casserole, extended time as needed to cooked completely & a temp placed in the centre, reading 165 degrees.

Nutritional Values:

Calories: 398 g, Fat: 10 g, Carbs: 47 g, Protein: 34 g, Iron: 2 mg

Spicy Beef and Bell Pepper Stir-Fry

Get ready for an enticing combination of flavours that will excite your tongue and satisfy your demands. The recipe will crank up the heat. This iron-rich meal features tender beef, bright bell peppers, and a spicy concoction of spices.

Prep Time: 10 min   **Cook Time: 10 mins**   **Servings: 4**

Ingredients:

15 g minced ginger (1 tbsp)	10 ml chili garlic sauce (2 tsp)
360 g flank steak (12 oz)	15 ml canola oil (1 tbsp)
1 yellow bell pepper	4 green onions
10 g toasted sesame seeds (2 tsp)	45 ml lower-sodium soy sauce (3 tbsp)
18 g rice wine vinegar (1 ½ tbsp)	
1 red bell pepper	

Instructions:

1. At a medium high flame, warm a big skillet. Pour oil to the pan and stir to coat.
2. Put the steak to the pan and broil it on one side, for about two mins.
3. While stirring frequently, sauté the bell pepper, till beef gets its pink texture, cook for about two mins.
4. Take the meat mixture out of the pan. In the pan, put ginger, soy sauce, chili garlic sauce and vinegar and come to a boil.
5. Till almost thickened, cook for about one min.

6. Stir completely to coat the pan after adding the onions with beef mixture.
7. Drizzle sesame seeds on top.

Nutritional Values:

Calories: 216 g, Fat: 11.5 g, Carbs: 7.7 g, Protein: 20.8 g, Iron: 3 mg

Grilled Chicken with Arugula Pesto

Brace up for an explosion of nutrition and pleasure. Improve your evening with grilled chicken with arugula pesto. The flavourful rocket pesto goes well with tender, grilled chicken.

Prep Time: 25 min   Cook Time: 25 mins   Servings: 4

Ingredients:

60 g toasted pine nuts (¼ cup)	4 g kosher salt (¾ tsp)
40 ml lemon juice (8 tsp)	4 boneless chicken breast halves
500 g packed arugula (2 ½ cups)	1 garlic clove
4 g ground pepper (¾ tsp)	222 ml olive oil (¾ cup plus 3 tbsp)
2 lb fingerling potatoes (32 oz)	
60 g grated Parmigiano-Reggiano cheese (¼ cup)	

Instructions:

1. Blend cheese, ¾ of tsp of pepper & salt, garlic, arugula and pine nuts in the handheld blender for about thirty secs, till roughly minced.
2. Blend for about a min, till creamy, while gently steam in the ¾ cup of olive oil. Keep the pesto separate.
3. Heat an indoor electric grill to 375 F on one side & 400 F on the other side.
4. For each chicken breast, make a small pocket for stretched the skin with your hands.
5. Place two Tbsp of pesto into every pocket then with your fingertips to evenly spread the pesto out.

6. For about six mins, sauté the chicken, side down the chicken at 400 F. Grill the chicken for an additional five mins.
7. Turning it around 180 degrees, till crispy and the skin is golden brown in colour. In order to ensure equal browning, rotate the chicken and continue to grill it for an additional twelve to fifteen mins.
8. In the meantime, combine the three Tbsp of pepper, salt, olive oil and potatoes in a bowl.
9. Grill the potatoes for every nine to fifteen mins, turning the potatoes around every four mins.
10. In addition to the extra pesto, serve the chicken with potatoes.

Nutritional Values:

Calories: 671 g, Fat: 37 g, Carbs: 46 g, Protein: 35 g, Iron: 3.6 mg

Shrimp Enchiladas

Adding these Iron rich shrimp enchiladas to the meal will spice it up. A tempting mix of taste plus nutrition is achieved in tortillas by exquisite prawns, flavourful seasonings and elements that are high in iron. Enjoy a fiesta of flavours that will satisfy your hunger and supply your body.

Prep Time: 05 min   Cook Time: 25 mins   Servings: 6

Ingredients:

240 g chopped onion (1 cup)	10 g minced garlic (2 tsp)
2.5 g ground cumin (1/2 tsp)	300 g hatch green chile enchilada sauce with roasted garlic (10 oz)
240 g shredded pepper Jack cheese (8 oz)	5 g old bay seasoning (1 tsp)
15 g lime juice (1 tbsp)	12 corn tortillas
Cilantro leaves for garnish	120 g hatch diced green chiles (4 oz)
1 lb cooked medium shrimp (16 oz)	

Instructions:

1. Combine green chilies, ½ the shredded cheese, minced garlic, cooked prawns, lime juice, old bay seasoning, onions and cumin in the bowl.
2. Mix together all ingredients till completely blended. Place flat service and roll corn tortillas.
3. Put the shrimp mixture inside. Roll up the enchiladas and place them in a casserole dish.

4. Roast the garlic and toss with hatch green Chile enchilada sauce. Enchilada with the extra cheese on top.
5. Warm up the oven to 400 F/200 C, then bake for twenty-five mins till cheese is melted.
6. Add cilantro leaves for garnish.

Nutritional Values:

Calories: 907 g, Fat: 55 g, Carbs: 41 g, Protein: 52 g, Iron: 2.7 mg

Crustless Ham and Collard Greens Quiche

Experience crustless ham with collard greens quiche to explore the perfect balance of flavours. This amazing dinner recipe blends iron-rich collard greens, savoury ham and other healthy ingredients to make a guilt-free quiche that satisfies cravings while nourishing the body. Sink into a chunk of wholesome desire.

Prep Time: 15 min   Cook Time: 45 mins   Servings: 6

Ingredients:

240 g milk (1 cup)	180 g shredded pepper Jack cheese (1 ½ cups)
18 g olive oil (1 ½ tsp)	2 large eggs
60 g all-purpose baking mix (1/2 cup)	120 g diced onion (1/2 cup)
½ pkg frozen chopped collard greens	
2 g salt (1/4 tsp)	
240 g chopped baked ham (1 cup)	

Instructions:

1. Heat the oven to 400 F/200 C.
2. Take a skillet, at moderate flame, Start cooking the meat in heated oil for about five mins, till it is golden brown.
3. Mix the collards and onion and start cooking for about five mins, till the onion is soft and the liquid has evaporated.
4. Take a pie plate, lightly oiled, put half of the collard mixture with ¾ of cheese cup on top.

5. Layers once more times. Combine the extra ingredients and milk till it becomes moisture.
6. In pie plate, add cheese mix and collard on top.
7. Bake for twenty-five to thirty mins in a preheated oven till a knife placed in centre comes out clean.
8. Before serving, allow ten mins to cool down.

Nutritional Values:

Calories: 342 g, Fat: 28 g, Carbs: 7 g, Protein: 16 g, Iron: 1 mg

Steak with Chipotle-Lime Chimichurri

With steak and chipotle-lime chimichurri, spice up your evening. A delicious, iron rich chimichurri sauce with a fiery chipotle-lime base meets a juicy steak. This hot treat fills your stomach while also satisfying your wants for something nutritious.

Prep Time: 15 min   Cook Time: 15 mins   Servings: 8

Ingredients:

4 g pepper (3/4 tsp)	2 lb beef flat iron steaks (32 oz)
120 ml lime juice (1/4 cup)	120 ml olive oil (1/2 cup)
½ chopped red onion	7 g salt (1 ¼ tsp)
5 garlic cloves	54 cilantro leaves (1 ½ cups)
60 ml white wine vinegar (1/4 cup)	5 g grated lime zest (1 tsp)
15 g dried oregano (3 tsp)	60 g parsley leaves (2 cups)

Instructions:

1. Put the first five ingredients in a food processer for chimichurri and blend till finely minced.
2. Process till well combined the lime juice, one-fourth of tsp of pepper, half of tsp of salt, lemon zest, vinegar and oil.
3. Place to a bowl and keep chilled under cover till serving. Add steaks with the extra pepper and salt.
4. Grill the meat for about five to eight mins at medium heat under cover, till you prefer the level of completion.
5. Before slicing, allow for five mins rest.
6. Add chimichurri and serve.

Nutritional Values:

Calories: 336 g, Fat: 26 g, Carbs: 4 g, Protein: 22 g, Iron: 4 mg

Chicken & Mushroom Puff Pastry Bundles

"With chicken & mushroom puff pastry bundles, unwrap a bundle of flavour. These golden treats have flaky puff pastry, delicate chicken, savoury mushrooms, and iron-rich ingredients.

Prep Time: 20 min   Cook Time: 30 mins   Servings: 4

Ingredients:

2 pieces boneless chicken breasts	28 g dijon mustard (2 tbsp)
240 g sliced mushrooms (8 oz)	30 g butter (2 tbsp)
15 g chopped thyme (1/8 cup)	1 small onion
115 g brick-style plain cream cheese (4 oz)	2 cloves garlic
60 g grated Parmesan cheese (1/4 cup)	15 g olive oil (1 tbsp)
30 g chopped chives (2 tbsp)	2 pre-rolled frozen puff pastry sheets
2.5 g each pepper & salt (1/2 tsp)	1 egg

Instructions:

1. Take the chicken out of the refrigerator and allow it at room temp. for ten mins.
2. Add half of the pepper and salt in it. Warm the oil and sauté the chicken for about five to seven mins in a big skillet at medium flame, till well done.

3. Place on a platter and keep. Sauté onion, pepper, salt, garlic, mushrooms and thyme for six to eight mins. Add the mushrooms mix to the pan and chicken again.

4. Set the oven to 400 F. Mustard and cream cheese are combined using mixer, till well combined.

5. Chives and parmesan cheese are then added. Put puff pastry on lightly dusted surface.

6. Make four squares out of each sheet and egg wash the edges. In centre of every square, pour 1 Tbsp of cream cheese mixture.

7. Chicken mixture and mushrooms are added on top. Bring the pastry's corners to the centre and press them together. Apply the leftover egg wash to the brush.

8. Cover the baking dish using parchment paper then place on it and start baking for about ten to fifteen mins, till it gives golden colour.

Nutritional Values:

Calories: 642 g, Fat: 45 g, Carbs: 33 g, Protein: 26 g, Iron: 3 mg

Honey-Beer Braised Ribs

Enjoy honey-beer braised ribs for a sweet and savoury symphony. These tender ribs are filled with iron-rich ingredients, slow-cooked to perfection, and drizzled with a delicious honey-beer glaze. Prepare yourself for a mouthwatering feast that will feed your body and satisfy your cravings.

Prep Time: 3 ½ hours   Cook Time: 10 mins   Servings: 6

Ingredients:

2.45 g pepper (1 tsp)	110 g brown sugar (1/2 cup)
85 g honey (1/4 cup)	510 g BBC sauce (18 oz)
3.70 g salt (3/4 tsp)	
2.70 kg pork baby back ribs (6 lb)	
60 ml cider vinegar (1/4 cup)	
355 ml ruby mild ale (12 oz)	

Instructions:

1. Rub the ribs with the mixture of pepper, brown sugar and salt.
2. In a pan roasting pan, put the ribs on a rack with bone side down. Add honey on top.
3. Pour vinegar and ruby mild ale around the ribs.
4. Over the ribs, apply some of the beef mixture with a spoon.
5. Bake for about one hour at 160 C with a foil that is well sealed.
6. Bake for an additional two hours till soften with the heat reduced to 120 C.

7. By using long-handled tongs, nourishing the paper towel with cooking oil, light cover the grill rack. Remove the ribs.
8. Grill for about ten to fifteen mins at a medium flame, covered, till browned, turning regularly and baste with Barbecue sauce.
9. With the leftover Barbecue sauce, serve.

Nutritional Values:

Calories: 531 g, Fat: 27 g, Carbs: 11 g, Protein: 53 g, Iron: 6.1 mg

Grilled Salmon with Lemon Garlic Butter

Prep Time: 10 mins   Cook Time: 25 mins   Servings: 4

Ingredients:

Pepper & salt to taste	2.5 g zest of 1 lemon (1/2 tsp)
4 salmon fillets	115 g butter (1/2 cup)
15 ml olive oil (1 tbsp)	4 g minced garlic (1 tsp)
Lemon garlic butter	
10 g chopped herbs (2 tsp)	
1.25 g salt (1/4 tsp)	

Instructions:

1. Mix lemon zest, softened butter, garlic, salt and herbs together.
2. Use a fork to mix by mashing. With a paper towel, pat the salmon dry.
3. Drizzle oil over it then sprinkle with pepper and salt lightly.
4. Cook salmon for about eight mins at medium flame, after turning it over, grill for an additional four to six mins.
5. Take the salmon out of the heat with a spoonful of lemon-garlic butter on top as soon as possible. Enjoy.

Nutritional Values:

Calories: 293 g, Fat: 15 g, Carbs: 2 g, Protein: 35 g, Iron: 1.5 mg

Baked Beans with Ground Beef

Enjoy the perfect balance of nutrition and pleasure in baked beans with ground beef. This filling recipe, which combines savoury baked beans, soft ground beef, and other iron-rich ingredients, will fuel your body and satisfy your appetites. Set yourself for a cozy experience!

Prep Time: 15 min **Cook Time: 10 mins** **Servings: 6**

Ingredients:

237 ml water (1 cup)	180 g ketchup
1.25 g salt (1/4 tsp)	850 g no-salt-added navy beans (30 oz)
455 g lean ground beef (1 lb)	5 g dijon mustard (1 tsp)
85 g molasses (1/4 cup)	15 g chopped chives for garnish (1/4 cup)
15 ml olive oil (1tbsp)	1 chopped onion
2.5 g garlic powder (1/2 tsp)	

Instructions:

1. Take a saucepan, warm the oil at moderate high flame.
2. Put ground beef & onion. Cook for about five mins, till the beef is no more pink and the onion is soft, tossing and crumbling the beef with spatula.
3. Stir to a simmer the molasses, salt, ketchup, beans, garlic powder, water and mustard.
4. Cook for about five to eight mins, turn down the flame to normal and start cook till the mixture starts bubbling and gets thick.

5. If liked, add chives, as a garnish.

Nutritional Values:

Calories: 346 g, Fat: 10 g, Carbs: 41 g, Protein: 23 g, Iron: 4 mg

Angel Chicken

Prepare to taste angelic flavours. Enjoy our Iron rich angel chicken's delicious flavours. In this wonderful recipe, juicy chicken is smothered in a creamy sauce flavoured with savoury herbs and foods high in iron. Please with a dinner that will meets your needs and also nourishing your body.

Prep Time: 15 min   **Cook Time: 15 mins**   **Servings: 4**

Ingredients:

80 g dried cherries (1/2 cup)	340 g boneless chicken breasts (3/4 lb)
225 g angel hair pasta (8 oz)	2.5 g salt (1/2 tsp)
30 g pine nuts (1/4 cup)	170 g baby spinach (6 oz.)
0.30 g pepper (1/8 tsp)	37 g chopped pecans (1/3 cup)
7.80 g cornstarch (1 tbsp)	15 ml olive oil (1 tbsp)
45 g shredded parmesan cheese (1/2 cup)	0.60 g ground nutmeg (1/4 tsp)

Instructions:

1. As directed to the package instructions, cook the pasta till almost cooked.
2. Mix pepper, salt and chicken with cornstarch in a bowl.
3. Warm the oil at a moderate flame in a big skillet.
4. Put the chicken mix and cook for about five to seven mins till the meat is no more pink.

5. Cook for about three to four mins after adding the cherries and the spinach till the spinach has wilted.
6. After rinsing the pasta, save three-fourth cup of the cooking liquid. Put the pasta in a big bowl.
7. Toss the spaghetti with nutmeg to mix.
8. Add enough of the saved pasta water to the spaghetti to make it moist.
9. Add the parmesan, pine nuts, chicken mixture and pecan to the spaghetti as a garnish. Serve right away.

Nutritional Values:

Calories: 608 g, Fat: 21 g, Carbs: 64 g, Protein: 37 g, Iron: 2 mg

Quick Tacos Al Pastor

Take a trip filled with flavour with our Iron-Rich Quick Tacos Al Pastor. These salty tacos fulfil your meals, better your health, and take your taste senses to Mexican street food ecstasy thanks to the combination of succulent marinated pork, vivid spices, and iron rich foods.

Prep Time: 10 min   **Cook Time: 18 mins**   **Servings: 4**

Ingredients:

680 g ground pork (1 ½ lb)	6.8 g paprika (1 ½ tsp)
2 g onion powder (1/2 tsp)	9.85 g salt (2 tsp)
As needed Cilantro	170 g pineapple (6 oz.)
30 ml olive oil (2 tbsp)	8 g garlic powder (1 ½ tsp)
2.45 g pepper (1/2 tsp)	As Needed Cotija, or Queso Fresco Cheese
As needed Onions	35 g tomato paste (2 tbsp)
2 minced Cloves garlic	12 soft corn tortillas
4.90 g chipotle powder (1 tsp)	4.5 g cumin powder (1 tsp)
80 g diced onion (3 oz)	

Instructions:

1. Warming the corn tortillas in a big skillet at a medium flame.
2. Cook the tortilla in a skillet for about forty-five secs before turning it and continuing cooking for a further forty-five secs.

16

3. Take out of the pan and pour in a towel. Cover them & repeat with leftover tortillas.
4. Spray in the oil in a big skillet at normal flame.
5. Combine all of the seasoning, ground pork and onions. As the meat cooks, crumbled it.
6. Stirring constantly, mix tomato paste and minced garlic to the pan.
7. Now include the pineapple into the mixture. Serve on heated tortillas after taken off the heat.
8. Add sauces and topping on top, whatever you liked. Enjoy!

Nutritional Values:

Calories: 350 g, Fat: 22 g, Carbs: 16 g, Protein: 19 g, Iron: 2 mg

Caribbean Slow Cooker Pot Roast

Transport your pallet and senses to the Caribbean's sun-drenched islands with slow cooker pot roast. This irresistible dish combines succulent pot roast with island-inspired spices and iron-rich ingredients to create a culinary voyage that satisfies cravings and feeds the body. Enjoy for an experience of paradise.

Prep Time: 10 min   Cook Time: 8 hours 20 mins   Servings: 6

Ingredients:

5.70 g kosher salt (1 tsp)	425 g tomato sauce (1 ¾ cups)
3 cloves garlic	30 ml vegetable oil (2 tbsp)
3 g ground cumin (1/2 tsp)	2 g coriander (1/2 tsp)
1.35 kg boneless beef chuck roast (48 oz)	12.5 g brown sugar (1 tbsp)
0.61 g ground cinnamon (1/8 tsp)	Zest of 1 orange
1 diced jalapeno pepper	1.5 g oregano (1/8 tsp)
7.81 g all purpose flour (1/2 tbsp)	240 g chopped red onion (1 cup)

Instructions:

1. Warm the oil at a medium high flame in a big skillet.
2. Rotating frequently, is necessary to evenly brown the roast.
3. In a slow cooker, put the roast that holds 4-quarts.
4. In the same pan that was used to brown ha roast, put the garlic, jalapenos and onions.

5. Cook, stirring frequently, till the onions begin to soften. While sautéing, remove any brown parts from the roast.
6. Exclude the tomato sauce, put all of the leftover ingredients and stir to mix well.
7. In the meantime, the tomato sauce is added and simmer for a min, and stir to mix.
8. On top of the roast, pour the sauce in a slow cooker. Flip the roast to ensure that the sauce is applied on every side.
9. For eight hours, simmer on low setting under cover.
10. Before slicing, take the roast out and let it rest for about five mins.
11. After removing any fat, serve the sauce in a slow cooker & also with the slice roast.

Nutritional Values:

Calories: 589.4 g, Fat: 36.7 g, Carbs: 24.3 g, Protein: 39.2 g, Iron: 4.5 mg

Chicken Thighs with Shallots and Spinach

With iron rich chicken thighs with shallots and spinach, enjoy an abundance of flavours. A wonderful melody of texture and nutrition is created by the mingling of tender chicken thighs with vivid spinach, caramelized shallots, and iron-rich components, enhancing your dining experience.

Prep Time: 15 min   Cook Time: 15 mins   Servings: 6

Ingredients:

2.45 g pepper (1/2 tsp)	2.45 g seasoned salt (1/2 tsp)
285 g spinach (1 cup)	80 ml white wine (1 1/8 cup)
680 g boneless chicken thighs (1 ½ lb)	1.25 g salt (1/4 tsp)
7.5 ml olive oil (1 1/2 tsp)	
60 g reduced-fat sour cream (1/4 cup)	
4 shallots thinly sliced	

Instructions:

1. With pepper & salt to taste, season the chicken. Heat up the oil at moderate flame in a skillet.
2. Cook for about six mins on every side, after adding the chicken, till a thermometer measures 170 degrees.
3. Take out of the pan and keep heated. Shallots are cooked and stirred in the same pan till soft.

4. Bring to a simmer, after adding the wine. Cook the wine, till it becomes half.
5. Salt and spinach are then cooked and stirred till the spinach has wilted.
6. Serve the chicken, after adding in the sour cream.
7. Cool the spinach combination and the spinach before adding the sour cream.
8. In freezers vessels, freeze it. To use, defrost slightly in the fridge at night.
9. Stirring periodically, heat up slowly in a covered skillet till a thermometer placed in the chicken gives reading 170 degrees.
10. Add the sour cream.

Nutritional Values:

Calories: 223 g, Fat: 10 g, Carbs: 7 g, Protein: 23 g, Iron: 3 mg

Conga Lime Pork

"Conga lime pork, which is rich in iron, will have you dancing to its energetic flavours. With sour lime, iron rich vegetables, and an abundance of Latin spices, delicate pork is infused in this zesty recipe. Dinner that relies your body while taking the fiesta to your plate.

Prep Time: 10 min   Cook Time: 15 mins   Servings: 4

Ingredients:

20 g molasses (4 tsp)	1 chipotle pepper in adobo sauce
455 g boneless pork chops (1 lb)	15 ml olive oil (1 tbsp)
½ chopped onion	4 garlic cloves
30 ml lime juice (2 tbsp)	5.70 g salt (1 tsp)
60 ml water (1/4 cup)	
2.45 g black pepper (½ tsp)	

Instructions:

1. Take a skillet, hot the olive oil at moderate high flame.
2. Mix pepper & salt with pork chops together.
3. Cook for about three to four mins after placing in the skillet till cooked completely.
4. In the same skillet, put the garlic & onions and simmer for about three mins till the onion becomes transparent.
5. Pour the chipotle peppers, water and molasses in to the skillet.
6. Stir to lift the browned bits out of the pan's bottom.
7. Boil for a moment them turn down the flame and start cooking for five mins.

8. Mix the pork chops and lime juice to the pan.
9. Cook for a few mins, till the pork chops are coated with the sauce.

Nutritional Values:

Calories: 514 g, Fat: 23 g, Carbs: 46 g, Protein: 31 g, Iron: 3 mg

Hawaiian Teriyaki Chicken Skewers

"With iron rich Hawaiian teriyaki chicken skewers, travel your taste detects to a tropical world. Juicy chicken, luscious pineapple, and iron rich components are incorporated in these flavour-packed skewers to create a wonderful feast that fulfils desires while replenishing the body. I say, "Hail to deliciousness!"

Prep Time: 15 min   Cook Time: 10 mins   Servings: 4

Ingredients:

110 g brown sugar (½ cup)	1 chopped red bell pepper
2 minced garlic cloves	340 g pineapple (12 oz)
8 g cornstarch (1 ½ tsp)	1.25 g pepper (1/4 tsp)
120 ml soy sauce (1/2 cup)	1 chopped red bell pepper
1 chopped red onion	2.45 g salt (1/2 tsp)
4 boneless chicken breasts	green onions for garnish
15 ml water (1 tbsp)	1 chopped green bell pepper
60 ml pineapple juice (1/4 cup)	

Instructions:

1. Mix together the pepper, garlic, soy sauce, salt, brown sugar and pineapple juice in a small sauce pan.
2. Further add the water and cornstarch in the bowl. Toss into mixture.
3. Simmer for a moment & continue to cook for about one to three mins till the mix slightly thick.
4. Take away from heat then set aside one-fourth cup of the sauce.

5. Refrigerate the chicken for at least thirty mins while it marinates in the sauce.
6. Together with the pineapple, peppers and onion, skewers the chicken.
7. Grill the meat for about eight to ten mins, till is done.
8. Take off the grill then baste with the sauce you served. If required, add green onions as a garnish.

Nutritional Values:

Calories: 248 g, Fat: 3 g, Carbs: 30 g, Protein: 26 g, Iron: 1.5 mg

Creamy Fontina Cheese Pasta

Enjoy the silky richness of pasta with iron rich cream and fontina cheese. This delightful dish mixes perfectly cooked pasta with a creamy, iron loaded fontina cheese sauce to create a symphony of tastes that accomplishes your appetites while sustaining your health. Ready to enjoy for a pasta feast!

Prep Time: 05 min   **Cook Time: 10 mins**   **Servings: 6**

Ingredients:

56.5 g unsalted butter (1/4 cup)	Black pepper to taste
225 g shredded fontina (1 cup)	Salt to taste
454 g pasta (17 oz)	

Instructions:

1. Prepare pasta till it is cooked through by bringing a saucepan of salted water to a simmer.
2. Return pasta to the saucepan after draining.
3. Add cheese & butter then season to taste.
4. Serve right away.

Nutritional Values:

Calories: 519 g, Fat: 22 g, Carbs: 57 g, Protein: 21 g, Iron: 1.5 mg

Applesauce Pork Tenderloin Recipe

"Iron rich apple puree pork tenderloin will boost your supper experience. This delightful dish produces an appealing flavour mix that sustains your body and fulfils your taste buds by combining juicy pork tenderloin with applesauce's natural sweetness and iron-rich components.

Prep Time: 15 min   Cook Time: 1 hour 45 mins   Servings: 6

Ingredients:

30 ml vegetable oil (6 tsp)	2 sprigs rosemary
55 g brown sugar (1/4 cup)	240 g unsweetened applesauce (1 cup)
42 g honey (2 tbsp)	2.45 g salt (1/2 tsp)
1.25 g pepper (1/2 tsp)	
905 g pork tenderloin (32 oz)	
45 g dijon mustard (3 tbsp)	

Instructions:

1. Heat the oven to 400 F/200 C.
2. Put pepper and salt on the pork.
3. Warm up the vegetables at moderate heat in a skillet.
4. In a skillet, brown the toast on each side. Take a roasting pan, place the roast.
5. Spread the roasted meat with the mixture of brown sugar, honey, applesauce and mustard.
6. A thermometer placed in the tenderloin indicate 155 degrees after thirty to forty mins of baking with the lid off.

7. Top with rosemary.

Nutritional Values:

Calories: 300 g, Fat: 10 g, Carbs: 20 g, Protein: 32 g, Iron: 2 mg

Chicken and vegetable tagine

"Iron rich chicken and vegetable tagine will take your taste buds on an extravagant adventure with its mouthwatering mix of the succulent chicken, vivid veggies, and iron rich components. This delightful dinner will transport you to Morocco and nourish your taste buds while replenishing your body.

Prep Time: 15 min   **Cook Time: 1 hour 20 mins**   **Servings: 6**

Ingredients:

1 large carrot	400 g chicken breast (14.1 oz)
160 g chopped pumpkin (6 oz.)	1 small birds eye chili
425 g chickpeas (15 oz.)	½ red capsicum
4.5 g ras el hanout (1 tsp)	410 g diced tomatoes (14.5 oz)
Pepper and salt to taste	240 g chicken stock (1 cup)
2 garlic cloves	1 sliced red onion
2.45 g cinnamon (1/2 tsp)	

Instructions:

1. Heat your tagine to 60 F in a chilly oven.
2. When the chicken is browned (a few mins), remove it from the saucepan after adding twelve Tbsp of olive oil to the big pot.
3. Till you prepared the vegetables, put aside.
4. Before adding the chili, onion and garlic, warm the remaining half of the olive oil in the same saucepan.

5. Gently fry till transparent onions. Saute for thirty secs after adding the cinnamon and ras el hanout.
6. Diced tomatoes and chickpeas are then added and combine well.
7. Season with salt and pepper after adding the pumpkin, chicken stock, carrot, reserved chicken, potato and capsicum.
8. Mix everything properly. Fill with the vegetable mix and the chicken before removing the tagine from the oven.
9. Return the tagine to the oven after covering it with the lid.
10. Till they are cooked well, cook the chicken & vegetables for about sixty to eighty mins.
11. Serve with the sides of your choice.

Nutritional Values:

Calories: 131 g, Fat: 131 g, Carbs: 11 g, Protein: 17 g, Iron: 2 mg

Hamburger Steak with Onions and Gravy

The tempting mix of juicy hamburger steak, sauteed onions, and a delicious iron loaded gravy will raise the standard of your dinner with "iron rich hamburger steak with onions and gravy." This nourishing dish is a fantastic crowd-pleaser because it replenishes you while satisfying your body needs.

Prep Time: 15 min   Cook Time: 25 mins   Servings: 4

Ingredients:

Bread crumbs (1/4 cup)	450 g ground beef (1 lb.)
1 egg	5 ml Worcestershire sauce (1 tsp)
2.5 g seasoned salt (1/2 tsp)	3 g onion powder (1/2 tsp)
2.5 g garlic powder (1/2 tsp)	0.6 g ground black pepper (1/8 tsp)
15 ml vegetable oil (1 tbsp)	240 g beef broth (1 cup)
30 g all-purpose flour (2 tbsp)	14 g cooking sherry (1 tbsp)
60 g sliced onion (1 cup)	

Instructions:

1. Take a bowl, combine the Worcestershire sauce, garlic powder, ground beef, pepper, egg, salt and bread crumbs.
2. Form eight balls, then patties by spreading out.
3. Take a skillet, warm oil at a medium flame.
4. Cook for about four mins per side, after adding onion and patties, till the patties are beautifully browned.

5. Place beef patties on a platter and keep them warm. Over the onions & dripping in the skillet, add flour.
6. With a fork, whisk in the flour, scraping any remaining beef portions from the skillet's bottom as you go.
7. Add sherry in broth gently. Use seasoned salt while seasoning.
8. At medium low heat, cook for about five mins, whisk, till the gravy thickens up.
9. Return patties to the gravy, cover and broil for about fifteen mins till well done.

Nutritional Values:

Calories: 319 g, Fat: 19 g, Carbs: 14 g, Protein: 23 g, Iron: 3 mg

The Ultimate Pork Chops

"Iron rich ultimate pork chops are a pork lover's dream—a tempting meal that blends juicy, luscious chops with iron loaded components. This amazing dinner strengthens your body while satisfying your body requirements and boosting your dining experience to entirely different levels. Be ready to taste excellence!"

Prep Time: 05 min   **Cook Time: 10 mins + Chilling**   **Servings: 4**

Ingredients:

475 ml water (2 cups)	2 g cumin (1/2 tsp)
60 g kosher salt (4 tbsp)	2 g black pepper (1/2 tsp)
4 (1-inch thick) bone-in pork chops	22 g paprika (4 tsp)
50 g sugar (1/4 cup)	2 g ground mustard (1/2 tsp)
475 ml ice (2 cups)	2 g garlic powder (1/2 tsp)
Rub:	2 g chili powder (1/2 tsp)
2 g onion powder (1/2 tsp)	

Instructions:

1. Add water, salt & sugar in a big pan.
2. Cook for a short time at moderate flame to dissolve the salt & sugar.
3. Take out of the heat. To bring brine to room temperature, add ice.
4. Add pork chops and the cooled brine in a gallon-sized resealable plastic bag.
5. Lock bag. For eight to twelve hours, refrigerate. Take out pork chops of the brine.

6. Dry towel after rinsing. Add the rub's ingredients together.
7. Apply both sides to the pork chops.
8. Cook the pork chops after set the grill till they achieve an internal temp of 145 F.

Nutritional Values:

Calories: 1136 g, Fat: 79 g, Carbs: 11 g, Protein: 91 g, Iron: 4 mg

Easy Stuffed Flank Steak Pinwheels

Be inventive in the kitchen with our Iron rich easy stuffed flank steak pinwheels. With their soft flank steak blended in iron-rich foods, these amazing and tasty dishes satisfy both your taste sensed and your wish to eat healthily. Prepare yourself for a tasty feast.

Prep Time: 05 min   Cook Time: 35 mins   Servings: 4

Ingredients:

680 g steak (1 ½ lb)	
3.5 g seasoned salt (1/2 tsp)	
115 g baby spinach leaves (1 cup)	
10 ml olive oil (2 tsp)	
170 g chive & onion cream cheese (3/4 cup)	

Instructions:

1. Set the oven temperature at 350 F/180 C.
2. Line the baking sheet using aluminum foil.
3. Adjust the steak on a chopping board, season with olive oil and sprinkle using salt to taste.
4. Turn over the meat. Cover the steak with cream cheese & lay spinach leaves on top.
5. Roll the steak cautiously, sealing the seam with dental picks to keep the spiral together.

6. Put the rolled steak on the baking sheet, bake for about thirty-five mins till the inside temp achieves at least 145 F.
7. Take out of the pan & let stand for about five to ten mins.
8. Slice into an-inch thick slices after removing toothpicks.

Nutritional Values:

Calories: 409 g, Fat: 25 g, Carbs: 3 g, Protein: 41 g, Iron: 3 mg

Beef and Swede Stew

Iron rich beef and swede stew will take your taste senses on an appealing adventure thanks to its hearty mix of cooked beef, healthy swede, and iron rich components.

Prep Time: 15 min   Cook Time: 6 hours 15 mins   Servings: 4

Ingredients:

3 garlic cloves	2 onions
2.45 g cumin (1/2 tsp)	15 g tomato puree (3 tsp)
Pepper and salt, to taste	½ lemon zest
3 sprigs of rosemary, 2 on the stalk, 1 leaf picked & chopped	2-3 carrots, scrubbed and cut into chunks
15 ml olive oil (1 tbsp)	170 ml red wine, optional (¾ cup)
1 star anise	1 swede
2 bay leaves	1.30 lb grass-fed beef (2 ¾ cups)
550 ml beef stock (2 ½ cup)	
14.5 oz chopped tomatoes (2 cups)	

Instructions:

1. Set the oven to at 150 degrees C/ 302 F.
2. In a casserole dish with a lid, warm up the olive oil.

3. Put the onions and start cooking over low flame for approximately five mins till they become tender.
4. Then put the garlic & simmer for an additional min or two.
5. Bring to a boil all the additional ingredients with the exception of the minced rosemary and lemon zest.
6. While you are going out, you may cook it for longer by lowering the oven's temperature to 120°c, which will take approximately four hrs.
7. Cover the pan and set it in the oven to roast for about two and half hours.
8. Cook the beef for a little while longer if it's not yet tender.
9. For added flavour, top with lemon zest & chopped rosemary right before serving.
10. It is best served in bowls so that you can enjoy the flavourful sauce and leafy greens like kale or cavolo nero.

Nutritional Values:

Calories: 352 g, Fat: 15 g, Carbs: 20 g, Protein: 30 g, Iron: 4 mg

Easy Slow Cooker Roast Beef Recipe

Ready to enjoy delightful perfection with our Iron rich easy slow cooker roast beef. This mouthwatering dish blends succulent beef, tasty seasonings, and iron-rich components for a delicious and satisfying dinner. Set it and forget an easy cooking feast.

Prep Time: 10 min   Cook Time: 8 hours   Servings: 8

Ingredients:

300 ml can of French onion soup (1 ¼ cup)	
2.04 kg boneless chuck roast (70 oz)	
1 packet dry onion soup mix	
300 ml can of beef consommé (1 ¼ cup)	

Instructions:

1. In the slow cooker, put the roast.
2. Pour French onion soup and beef consommé over the meat.
3. Add some of the dry soup mix for onions.
4. Your supper will be ready in eight hours if you cover it and set the temperature to high.

Nutritional Values:

Calories: 426 g, Fat: 26 g, Carbs: 2 g, Protein: 44 g, Iron: 4.8 mg

Cheeseburger Pizza

Get ready for the pizza experience like no other. A delectable mix of two cherished classics, offers the best of both worlds with cheeseburger pizza. This salty treat satisfies your desires while adding a nutritious twist. It is topped with delicious ground beef, melting cheese, and iron rich components.

Prep Time: 15 min   **Cook Time: 15 mins**   **Servings: 6**

Ingredients:

120 ml ketchup (1/2 cup)	170 g shredded cheddar cheese (3/4 cup)
45 ml dill pickle juice (3 tbsp)	1 prebaked 12-inch pizza crust
80 g chopped dill pickle (1 cup)	120 g mayonnaise (1/2 cup)
150 g shredded lettuce (1 ¾ cup)	60 g prepared mustard (1/4 cup)
225 g ground beef (1 cup)	
40 g chopped onion (1/2 cup)	

Instructions:

1. Set the oven temperature at 425° F/ 220 C.
2. Cook the beef in the skillet at a moderate flame, breaking it up into crumbles, for three to four mins, till no longer pink. Then drain it.
3. Place the crust on a pizza pan or baking sheet not oiled.
4. Spread ketchup and mustard together over the crust.
5. Bake the ground beef for five mins.
6. Sprinkle with cheese and bake for a further eight to ten mins, till cheese is bubbling and crust is gently browned.

7. Add pickles, lettuce, & onions on top.
8. Top the pizza with mayonnaise and as much pickle juice as you like.

Nutritional Values:

Calories: 521 g, Fat: 32 g, Carbs: 36 g, Protein: 21 g, Iron: 5 mg

Chocolate Waffle

A divine fusion of rich cocoa and iron rich ingredients, up your meal game. These crispy-on-the-outside, fluffy-on-the-inside waffles give a pleasant chocolatey experience that fulfils your desires while giving you a nutritional boost. It's dessert joy, one bite at a time!"

Prep Time: 05 min   Cook Time: 05 mins   Servings: 4

Ingredients:

100 g sugar (1/2 cup)	50 g cocoa powder (1/2 cup)
9.85 g baking powder (2 tsp)	2 eggs
170 g chocolate chips (3/4 cup)	56.5 g butter (4 tbsp)
2.45 g salt (1/2 tsp)	180 g all-purpose flour (1 ½ cup)
235 ml milk (1 cup)	
2.45 g baking soda (1 tsp)	

Instructions:

1. Heat the waffle maker.
2. Take a bowl, add the baking flour, sugar, cocoa, salt and flour, mix them together.
3. Add the eggs, milk and butter till incorporate.
4. Combine with chocolate chips.
5. Take almost one cup of batter, scoop it out and place it into the greased waffle maker.
6. Cook it for a few mins or till golden brown.

Nutritional Values:

Calories: 689 g, Fat: 28 g, Carbs: 102 g, Protein: 14 g, Iron: 5 mg

Double Chocolate Pancakes

A delicious approach to start your day with double chocolate pancakes. These lavish feasts offer a stack of fluffy, indulgent pancakes that fulfil your desires and give you a nutritional boost by combining rich chocolate with ingredients high in iron. The dessert meal has just been more delicious.

Prep Time: 05 min   Cook Time: 15 mins   Servings: 12

Ingredients:

2.45 g salt (1/2 tsp)	2 eggs
180 g all-purpose flour (1 ½ cup)	170 g semi crushed chocolate chips (3/4 cup)
4.95 ml vanilla extract (1 tsp)	20 g cocoa powder (4 tsp)
50 g sugar (3 tbsp)	
9.85 g baking powder (2 tsp)	
56.5 g butter (1/4 tsp)	

Instructions:

1. Take a bowl, whisk the sugar, salt, flour, baking powder, cocoa powder and together.
2. Take another bowl, mix the milk, butter, vanilla essence and eggs.
3. In the flour mixture, add the wet components into the well.
4. Stir till barely blended, don't over mix.
5. Finally, stir in the crumbled semi-sweet chocolate chips before adding the pancake mix.
6. Set the pancake mix aside for about five mins.

7. Set the skillet or griddle temperature at normal.
8. On a warm skillet or griddle, pour the pancake batter.
9. Cook for about one to two mins till tiny bubbles begin to arise.
10. By using a spatula, turn pancakes over & and cook for a further one to two mins till well done.
11. Get rid of the heat. Add diced strawberries and powdered sugar on top.

Nutritional Values:

Calories: 230 g, Fat: 4.5 g, Carbs: 41 g, Protein: 6 g, Iron: 3.4 mg

Chocolate Wafer Pie Crust

Get ready for absolute delight. Spend some time enjoying Iron thick Shoofly Pie, a dense, molasses-infused excitement. In order to make this classic Pennsylvania Dutch dessert, which meets desires while nourishing the body, iron rich foods are mixed with a crumbly, buttery crust.

Prep Time: 10 min   Cook Time: 01 mins   Servings: 8

Ingredients:

85 g unsalted butter (1/3 cup)	
255 g, 1 pkg chocolate wafers (1 cup)	

Instructions:

1. In a food processer, combine the butter and chocolate wafers.
2. Move the crumb mix to the pie dish, spread the crumbs with your fingers.
3. Place a bit of parchment paper in between your palms and the crumbs to flatten the crumbs.

Nutritional Values:

Calories: 881 g, Fat: 40.8 g, Carbs: 117.4 g, Protein: 11.1 g, Iron: 8 mg

Shoofly Pie

Prep Time: 10 min   Cook Time: 35 mins   Servings: 8

Ingredients:

4.95 g cinnamon (1 tsp)	100 g dark brown sugar (1/2 cup)
255 g molasses (1 cup)	1 single crust pie pastry
0.62 ml salt (1/8 tsp)	2.45 g nutmeg (1/2 tsp)
180 g flour (1 ½ cup)	175 ml boiling water (3/4 cup)
2.45 g baking soda (1/2 cup)	
113.5 g unsalted butter (1/2 cup)	

Instructions:

1. Set the oven temperature at 450 F/ 220 C.
2. Take a bowl, combine the sugar, nutmeg, salt, flour & cinnamon.
3. Using a pastry cutter, add the butter till the mixture resembles cornmeal.
4. Put into pastry shell after adding water, molasses & baking soda.
5. On the top, evenly distribute the crumb mix.
6. Bake for about fifteen mins, then continue baking for an additional twenty mins, till the mixture is thick and set.

Nutritional Values:

Calories: 440 g, Fat: 19 g, Carbs: 65 g, Protein: 3 g, Iron: 4 mg

Chocolate cake

Enjoy a slice of our delicious chocolate cake, a sweet confection that blends rich cocoa flavours with ingredients that are high in iron.

Prep Time: 20 min　　**Cook Time: 25 mins**　　**Servings: 8**

Ingredients:

For the sponge:	220 g caster sugar (1 cup)
4 large eggs	Small pinch salt
30 ml milk (3/4 cup)	15 g cocoa powder (3 tsp)
220 g unsalted butter (7.75 oz)	**For the ganache:**
4.95 ml vanilla extract (1 tsp)	10.60 oz dark chocolate (1 ¼ cup)
280 g flour (1 ½ cups)	10.60 fluid oz. double cream (1 ¼ cup)
4.95 g baking powder (1 tsp)	

Instructions:

1. Set the oven temp to 180 degrees F/240 C. Prepare cake tins by greasing & lining them.
2. Take a bowl, whisk the sugar & butter till they are light in colour. Mix together after adding all of the leftover sponge components, till thoroughly incorporate.
3. Smooth the top of the cake tins after dividing the mixture amongst them.

4. Till a skewer placed into the centre of the dish comes out clean, bake for about twenty to twenty-five mins. After baking, let the baked good cool in the pan for about ten mins then cool.
5. Assemble the ganache in the meantime. Dark chocolate is chopped into cubes and placed in a bowl while the double cream is gradually heated in a separate saucepan.
6. Pour the cream onto the dark chocolate when it is just about to boil, making sure to completely cover it. Let it stand for about two to three mins. Gently stir the ganache till is begins to come together and become glossy.
7. After allowing it rest for about ten mins, put the mixture into the refrigerator for around thirty mins, till it is spreadable. After the sponges have cooled, place one on a cake stand, topside up, and fill with one third of the ganache mix.
8. Top with the second sponge, topside up, and gently press down to seal it to the fling.
9. With the leftover mixture, frost the top of the cake by heaping it in the middle & spreading it out to the edges of the top sponge. Carefully cut into big slices & serve.

Nutritional Values:

Calories: 424 g, Fat: 22 g, Carbs: 58 g, Protein: 3.8 g, Iron: 3.3 mg

Easy Chiffon Pie

Try easy chiffon pie with iron for a light and airy touch. A scrumptious feast that melts in your tongue while nourishing your body, this amazing dessert mixes a lovely chiffon filling with iron-rich ingredients. Get ready for a slice of absolute dessert bliss.

Prep Time: 15 min　　　**Cook Time: 00 mins + chilling**　　　**Servings: 8**

Ingredients:

295 ml cold water (1 ¼ cup)	
1 reduced-fat graham cracker crust (9 inches)	
225 g frozen reduced-fat whipped topping (1 cup)	
8.5 g sugar-free strawberry gelatin (1 ½ tsp)	
340 g sliced strawberries (1 ½ cup)	
175 ml boiling water (3/4 cup)	

Instructions:

1. Take a bowl, add boiling water to dissolve gelatin.
2. Add cold water and stir till slightly thickened then refrigerate.
3. Stir in two cups of strawberries and the whipped topping.
4. Add liquid to the crust and adjust in the fridge for three hrs.
5. Add the leftover strawberries as a garnish.

Nutritional Values:

Calories: 138 g, Fat: 4 g, Carbs: 21 g, Protein: 2 g, Iron: 1 mg

Chocolate Cream Pie

Are you ready for a slice of pure chocolate pleasure? Enjoy chocolate cream pie and immerse yourself in velvety joy. Experience the silky-smooth chocolate filling that is the ideal complement to the crust's iron content. Your desires are sated and you get a nutritional boost from this delicious meal.

Prep Time: 10 min **Cook Time: 10 mins** **Servings: 4**

Ingredients:

96 g instant chocolate pudding mix (3.4 oz)	
1 frozen pie crust	
45 g mini chocolate chips (3 tbsp)	
475 ml cold milk (2 cups)	
225 g frozen whipped topping (1 cup)	

Instructions:

1. While preparing the pudding filling, bake the frozen pie crust according to the pack instructions and let it cool.
2. Take a bowl, mix custard & milk at low speed for two mins.
3. Add one cup of whipped topping and fold. Before serving, put the chill & crust into it for up to two hours.
4. Add the leftover chocolate chips & whipped topping on top, before serving.

Nutritional Values:

Calories: 1140 g, Fat: 63 g, Carbs: 128 g, Protein: 14 g, Iron: 6 mg

Fruit Cake

Enjoy a blend of tastes with iron rich fruit cake, a delicious masterpiece filled with a selection of dried fruits and iron rich components. This amazing dessert is anemia friendly and offers a blast of sweetness and nutrition in every bite.

Prep Time: 15 min   Cook Time: 40 mins   Servings: 8

Ingredients:

200 g sugar (1 cup)	180 g flour (1 ½ cups)
10 g baking powder (2 tsp)	60 g walnuts (½ cup)
230 g ashrafi (1 cup)	
4 eggs	
7/8 cup butter (14 tbsp)	
few drops vanilla essence	

Instructions:

1. Till frothy and light, beat the sugar & eggs.
2. Apply the butter now and start cooking till creamy.
3. Take another bowl, add the flour and the baking powder, mix together.
4. Combine the flour & butter mixtures.
5. Pour in the vanilla extract. Don't over fold when mixing.
6. Mix in the walnuts and ashrafi.
7. Bake the cake at 200 degrees C/400 F for thirty-five to forty mins till a toothpick placed near the centre comes out clean.
8. Take out from the oven, then set aside to cool. After that, slice it.

Nutritional Values:

Calories: 366 g, Fat: 10g, Carbs: 70 g, Protein: 3.3 g, Iron: 2.3 mg

Corn Custard

Experience a velvety delight. This dessert is a smooth fusion of sweet corn and iron rich ingredients. This decadent delight increases with its silky smoothness, delicate sweet cravings, and nourishing qualities, making it a delicious treat.

Prep Time: 20 min   **Cook Time: 60 mins**   **Servings: 6**

Ingredients:

4.2 g sugar (1 tsp)	28.35 g butter (1 oz.)
475 ml milk (2 cups)	32 g flour (1/4 cup)
2.45 g pepper (1/2 tsp)	5.70 g salt (1 tsp)
340 g corn kernels (1 ½ cup)	3 beaten eggs

Instructions:

1. Add maize & dry ingredients together.
2. Put butter, eggs and milk into it.
3. Put in a casserole or baking dish with butter that is sitting in a small pan of warm water.
4. Start baking for fifty to sixty mins at 350 F/180 C, till a knife placed in it comes out clean.

Nutritional Values:

Calories: 328g, Fat: 12.7 g, Carbs: 42.5 g, Protein: 10.88 g, Iron: 1.35 mg

Chocolate Pudding Pie

Enjoy the pure chocolate happiness with chocolate pudding pie. This delicious dessert will soothe your cravings while giving you a healthy nourishment. It blends rich chocolate tastes with vitamins that are high in iron.

Prep Time: 30 min   **Cook Time: 1-hour**   **Servings: 8**

Ingredients:

2 pkg. instant chocolate pudding and pie filling mix	
240 ml whipped topping (1 cup)	
285 g pie crusts (10 oz.)	
2 pkg instant chocolate pudding	

Instructions:

1. Take a pan and prepare the pie crust according to pack instructions.
2. Let it stand to cool for fifteen mins.
3. Add the milk & custard mix in a big bowl and beat for around two mins with a wire whisk.
4. Fill into the baked shell after it has cooled.
5. Move to the refrigerator for an hour.
6. Apply whipping cream at the top, then serve.
7. Garnish to taste. Keep in the fridge then serve.

Nutritional Values:

Calories: 327 g, Fat: 15 g, Carbs: 45 g, Protein: 4.7 g, Iron: 1.6 mg

Frozen Hot Chocolate

Prepare to sip and unwind? Transport to a winter wonderland with iron rich frozen hot chocolate. This cold dessert combines iron rich components with the comforting tastes of hot chocolate to produce an enticing and creamy treat that satisfies your sweet craving while nourishing your health.

Prep Time: 10 min　　　**Cook Time: 00 mins + chilling**　　　**Servings: 2**

Ingredients:

35 g sugar (1/8 cup)	10 g cocoa powder (2 tsp)
240 ml of whipped cream (1cup)	45 g chocolate chips (1/4 cup)
200 g mori-nu plus fortified tofu (1 cup)	
1 oz of chocolate syrup (2 tbsp)	
355 ml ice (1 1/3 cup)	
50 g of shaved chocolate (1/4 cup)	

Instructions:

1. Blend the cocoa powder, hot chocolate, tofu & sugar in the blender, till the mixture is completely lump free.
2. Blend in the ice till the mixture becomes slushy.
3. Then add shaved chocolate, whipped cream & chocolate syrup on top after pouring into dessert glasses.

Nutritional Values:

Calories: 750 g, Fat: 36 g, Carbs: 102 g, Protein: 12 g, Iron: 3 mg

Cake Batter Dip

Dive into a bowl of pure bliss with our Iron-Rich Cake Batter Dip. This happiness is guilt-free as it integrates foods that are high in iron with the flavours of cake batter to make a smooth, delicious dip that meets your sweet craving while feeding your body.

Prep Time: 15 min   **Cook Time: 00 mins + chilling**   **Servings: 2**

Ingredients:

89.45 ml milk (6 tbsp)	
67 g sprinkles (2.36 oz)	
113.5 g cream cheese (1/2 cup)	
90 g powdered sugar (3.17 oz)	
216 g funfetti cake mix (1 cup)	

Instructions:

1. Mix the cream cheese at medium-high speed in a stand mixer bowl by using the paddle attachment till it is smooth.
2. Add half of the heat-treated cake mix gradually while the mixer is set on slow.
3. Put half the milk, then mix by stirring.
4. Blend it after adding the leftover cake mix & milk.
5. Further add the powdered sugar and mix together.
6. Increase the mixer's speed when the powdered sugar is added to the bowl, blend everything together till smooth.
7. Use a spatula to fold the sprinkles. Serve with your preferred sides.

8. You can place it in the fridge for almost three or more days.

Nutritional Values:

Calories: 60 g, Fat: 2.5 g, Carbs: 8 g, Protein: 1 g, Iron: 1 mg

Cinnamon Roll Waffles with Cream Cheese Glaze

Enjoy the ideal combination of breakfast and dessert with iron rich cinnamon roll waffles. These yummy pastries have a cinnamon swoop, iron rich ingredients, and a thick cream cheese frosting that make them anemia-friendly treats that can cheer up any special occasion.

Prep Time: 25 min   Cook Time: 00 mins   Servings: 4

Ingredients:

60 ml milk (1/4 cup)	120 g powdered sugar (1 cup)
496 g cinnamon rolls with cream Cheese flavoured icing (17.5 oz)	
5 ml vanilla (1 tsp)	

Instructions:

1. After heating the waffle machine, spray it with cooking oil.
2. Divide the dough into five rolls and reserve the frosting.
3. Place one roll in the centre of the waffle maker for each waffle, then cover.
4. Bake the waffle for three to four mins, till golden brown and fully done.
5. In the meantime, mix the leftover icing, powdered sugar, vanilla, & milk in a small bowl and whisk till the glaze is smooth.
6. Serve hot waffles with glaze.

Nutritional Values:

Calories: 486.7 g, Fat: 35.4 g, Carbs: 22.5 g, Protein: 23.2 g, Iron: 3 mg

Cherry Cobbler

Give yourself a something nice with iron rich cherry cobbler, a sweet and tangy medley of juicy cherries, you can dig your teeth into a bowl of pure happiness. This dessert for people with anemia is a harmony of aromas that serve cravings while giving you a nutritious energy boost.

Prep Time: 15 min   Cook Time: 35 mins   Servings: 10

Ingredients:

22.20 ml lemon juice (1 ½ tbsp)	55 g brown sugar (1/2 cup)
50 g white sugar (1/4 cup)	**Crumb Topping:**
2.45 ml cinnamon (1/2 tsp)	2.45 ml salt (1/2 tsp)
900 g cherries, stemmed (2 lb)	170 g yellow cake mix (3/4 cup)
8.4 g cornstarch (1 ½ tsp)	85 g chilled butter (1/3 cup)
7.40 ml vanilla extract (1 ½ tsp)	55 g brown sugar (1/2 cup)
	4.93 g baking powder (1 tsp)

Instructions:

1. Set the oven temperature at 425 F/210 C.
2. Take off all of cherries' stems and seeds.
3. Take a dish, add cherries, cinnamon, lemon juice, corn flour, & sugars (brown, white) in it with the other ingredients.
4. Gently blend and toss. Fill a frying pan casserole with the cherry mixture.

5. Add yellow cake mix, salt, brown sugar, & baking powder together in the basin.
6. Stir and blend together. Mix the butter, stir it in with a fork till the combination resembles coarse crumbs.
7. Cover the cherries completely with crumb topping.
8. Bake for twenty-five to thirty-five mins, till the crumb topping is golden brown & the cherry juice is bubbling.
9. Serve and enjoy.

Nutritional Values:

Calories: 418 g, Fat: 8 g, Carbs: 83 g, Protein: 3 g, Iron: 2 mg

Rhubarb Pie

Explore the tangy-sweet taste of our Iron-Rich Rhubarb Pie. A tantalizing delicacy that combines rhubarb's vivid flavours with components that are rich in iron. Please with a rush of fruity sweetness with every chew that nourishes your body and stimulates your taste buds to more.

Prep Time: 25 min   Cook Time: 3 hours 20 mins   Servings: 8

Ingredients:

465 g sugar (2 ¼ cup)	2.5 g orange peel (1/2 tsp)
1.4 kg chopped rhubarb (3 ½ lb)	
400 g pie crusts (16 oz)	
85 g all-purpose flour (3/4 cup)	
15 g cold butter, optional (3 tsp)	
(2 Count), softened as directed on box	

Instructions:

1. Set the oven temperature at 425 F/210 C. Place one pie crust in the pie pan.
2. Take a bowl, mix flour, sugar, & orange peel in it. Add rhubarb and stir well.
3. Pour the mix into a platter with pastry on it. Sprinkle the rhubarb with the chopped-up butter.
4. Second crust on top; flute and seal. Make many slits in the top crust.

5. Wrap the edge of the crust with a pie crust shielding ring or with foil to avoid overbrowning.
6. Bake for fifty to fifty-five mins, removing foil for the final fifteen mins, till crust is brown and juice starts to bubbling through slits in crust.
7. Cool it for at least two hours on a cooling rack before serving.

Nutritional Values:

Calories: 470 g, Fat: 12 g, Carbs: 86 g, Protein: 3 g, Iron: 1.5 mg

Budin Puertorriqueno (Puerto Rican Bread Pudding)

Awaken your taste senses to the vivacious flavours of Puerto Rico. For a rich, anemia-friendly dessert that perfectly captures the island's gastronomic pleasures, this decadent dessert blends traditional herbs and spices, tropical fruits, and high in iron foods.

Prep Time: 30 min   Cook Time: 1 hour + chilling   Servings: 10

Ingredients:

6 slices stale sandwich loaf	14.80 ml vanilla essence (1 tbsp)
4.95 ml cinnamon (1 tsp)	240 g of raisins (1 cup)
A pinch of salt	200 g brown sugar (1 cup)
355 ml milk (1 ½ cup)	
1.25 ml nutmeg (1/8 tsp)	
3 eggs	

Instructions:

1. Take a bowl, put eggs and sugar in it, mix them.
2. Combine the salt, vanilla, spices, & milk in the batter.
3. Crumble the bread with your fingers, then stir it into the mixture.
4. Stir thoroughly till combined. Give it five to ten mins to set. Stir in the raisins to the batter.
5. Move the batter to a baking pan that buttered.
6. Bake for forty to forty-five mins, till the mixture is set, at 350 degrees F/180 C.
7. Serve chilled.

Nutritional Values:

Calories: 488 g, Fat: 16 g, Carbs: 75 g, Protein: 13 g, Iron: 3 mg

Tiger Nut Cake

Unleash your wild side and roar with joy as you tuck into our Iron-Rich Tiger Nut Cake. The specific flavours of tiger nuts, that having high iron and nutrients, are utilized in the special feasts to make a delightful treat that meets your sweet tooth while promoting your health.

Prep Time: 08 min   **Cook Time: 50 mins**   **Servings: 4**

Ingredients:

5.30 oz nut oil (3/4 cup)	250 g horchata (1 1/8 cup)
2 eggs	125 g powdered sugar (1 cup)
240 g flour (2 ¾ cups)	
200 g sugar (1 cup)	
0.70 oz baking powder (4 tsp)	
1.75 oz nut flour (3 tbsp)	

Instructions:

1. Set the oven's temperature to 180 degrees F/45 C.
2. Take a bowl, add eggs and sugar in a cream.
3. Lightly beat in the oil and horchata.
4. Add the sifted flour, nut flour, tiger & baking powder into the liquids.
5. Stir well to remove any lumps.
6. In a baking pan coated with parchment paper and oiled with tiger nut oil, pour the batter.
7. Bake the batter for almost thirty mins.

8. Remove from the oven, let it aside for cooling and top with powdered sugar before serving.

Nutritional Values:

Calories: 455 g, Fat: 1.2 g, Carbs: 95 g, Protein: 13 g, Iron: 5.8 mg

Sour Cream Raisin Pie

The iron rich sour cream raisin pie is going to send to you in the antiquity. This anemia-friendly feast mixes plump raisins and iron-rich components into a classic delight which soothes your heart and nurtures your body. It offers a silky-smooth pleasure with a bit of tartness.

Prep Time: 20 min   Cook Time: 50 mins   Servings: 8

Ingredients:

2.46 ml cinnamon (1/2 tsp)	1.25 ml kosher salt (1/8 tsp)
9 pastry shell	150 g light brown sugar (3/4 cup)
4.95 ml vanilla essence (1 tsp)	4.95 ml lemon juice (1 tsp)
3 eggs	240 ml sour cream (1 cup)
1.25 ml cloves (1/8 tsp)	
225 g raisins (1 cup)	

Instructions:

1. Set the oven's temperature to 350 F/180 C.
2. Boil some water in a kettle.
3. Put the vanilla in a bowl with the raisins.
4. Cover the raisins with the boiling water. Give it ten to fifteen mins heat. Start baking the pie crust in a preheated oven for ten mins,
5. Take a basin, add brown sugar, lemon juice, eggs, cloves, salt, cinnamon & sour cream in it and whisked together till smooth.
6. After draining, mix the raisins with the pie mixture and stir thoroughly.
7. Put the mixture into the pie dough that has already been baked.

8. Place the pie in the oven after placing it on a baking pan.
9. Bake the pie for thirty-five to forty mins, till it starts to colour.
10. When baking, the pie mixture will balloon up over the pie crust; but, when chilled, it will settle down into a beautiful custard. On a cooling rack, let the pie cool at room temperature.
11. Serve it refrigerated or at room temperature. Before serving, top with whipped cream, if you liked.

Nutritional Values:

Calories: 354 g, Fat: 13 g, Carbs: 54 g, Protein: 4 g, Iron: 2 mg

Easy banana cake

Get ready to go bananas for this mouthwatering easy banana cake that mixes the sweetness of ripe bananas with iron rich components. Juicy and savoury, this delightful delicacy is a sans guilt approach quench your sugar cravings and gives you the strength.

Prep Time: 15 min   **Cook Time: 45 mins**   **Servings: 12**

Ingredients:

150 g caster sugar (3/4 cup)	180 g flour (3/4 cup)
1 egg	
60 ml milk (1/4 cup)	
4.4 oz butter (¾ cup)	
2 bananas mashed	
5 ml vanilla extract (1 tsp)	

Instructions:

1. Take a pan, heat the vanilla, sugar, & butter till melt. Take off from the heat.
2. Mash the bananas, then add them and stir till incorporated.
3. Add the egg, then combine well.
4. Add the milk and gently fold it after stirring.
5. Bake for about forty mins at 170 F/40 C.

Nutritional Values:

Calories: 624 g, Fat: 53 g, Carbs: 4.6 g, Protein: 33 g, Iron: 3 mg

Bacardi rum cake

Cheers to a pleasant and energetic treat. Let your taste buds run with this anemia friendly Bacardi rum cake dessert. This delicious delicacy melds the richness of Bacardi rum with the iron rich ingredients to yield in a moist. The salty dessert which satisfies hunger and nourishes the body.

Prep Time: 30 min   **Cook Time: 1 hour 10 mins**   **Servings: 12**

Ingredients:

120 ml cold water (1/2 cup)	4 eggs
405 g yellow cake mix (14.25 oz)	200 g granulated sugar (1 cup)
120 g chopped pecans or walnuts (1 cup)	115 g butter (1/4 lb)
120 ml bacardi rum (1/2 cup)	120 ml wesson oil (1/2 cup)
95 g vanilla pudding mix (3.4 oz)	
60 ml water (1/4 cup)	

Instructions:

1. Set the oven temperature at 325 F/175 C.
2. Apply butter & flour on the tube pan.
3. Add the nuts at the lower side of pan.
4. Take the bowl, add cake mix, custard mix, oil, eggs, water, & half cup Bacardi in it.
5. Add batter in the nuts. Then place it aside for one hour to cool.
6. Apply glaze over the top and sides.

7. Let the glaze soak into the cake. Continue the process till glazing is finished.
8. Take a pan, melt the butter by heating it.
9. Add sugar and water and stir together. Start boiling for five mins.
10. Take off from the heat. Stir in the rum.

Nutritional Values:

Calories: 503 g, Fat: 3.63 g, Carbs: 105.6 g, Protein: 6.75 g, Iron: 2 mg

Spice Cake

Enjoy the delicious iron rich spice cake, comfortable, hot sour delicacy that strengthens your body and attracts your taste buds without making you seem terrible. This sweet dish is a delectable treat that fulfil your hunger and increase your energy as it is packed with iron rich components.

Prep Time: 10 min　　　**Cook Time: 40 mins**　　　**Servings: 4**

Ingredients:

0.6 g baking powder (1/8 tsp)	0.6 g nutmeg (1/8 tsp)
60 g salted butter (1/4 cup)	15 ml vegetable oil (1 tbsp)
0.6 g cloves (1/8 tsp)	1 large egg
1.2 ml vanilla extract (1/4 tsp)	60 ml milk (1/4 cup)
0.6 g salt (1/8 tsp)	0.6 g ground cinnamon (1/4 tsp)
150 g brown sugar (3/4 cup)	95 g all-purpose flour (3/4 cup)
0.6 g ginger (1/4 tsp)	

Instructions:

1. Set the temperature of oven at 350°F/180 C.
2. Apply butter on the baking dish.
3. Take a mixer, then combine the brown sugar & butter in the bowl.
4. Pour the oil, egg with vanilla extract and beat them well.
5. Take another bowl, combine the flour, ginger, salt, cloves, baking powder, and nutmeg.

6. Mix well the dry ingredients in the egg/butter mixture. Add the milk and stir together.
7. Put the batter into a baking pan and adjust it on a baking tray.
8. Start baking for forty to forty-five mins, till the top is browned.
9. Take out the baking dish and set it aside to chill.

Nutritional Values:

Calories: 370 g, Fat: 16 g, Carbs: 59 g, Protein: 5 g, Iron: 2 mg

Honey Nut Oatmeal Waffles

Honey nut oatmeal waffles are the secret remedy for a deliciously energizing dessert. Rise and shine with a serving of this delightful meal. These flaky waffles merge the relaxing aromas of honey and almonds with the goodness of iron making days well savoring.

Prep Time: 10 min   Cook Time: 15 mins   Servings: 12

Ingredients:

90 g old-fashioned oats (1 cup)	470 ml milk (2 cups)
2.5 ml (1/2 tsp)	10 g baking powder (2 tsp)
2 eggs	60 g unsalted butter (1/4 cup)
180 g whole wheat flour (1 ½ cup)	
40 g honey (2 tbsp)	
120 g chopped pecans or walnuts (1 cup)	

Instructions:

1. Take a basin, mix the flour, almonds, baking soda, oats & salt.
2. Take a bowl, mix the milk, butter, eggs & honey together.
3. Stir the liquid mixture into the flour mixture.
4. Warm the waffle iron. Apply a light coating of nonstick spray.
5. Pour one-third of batter onto the waffle iron, spread it, and bake it as directed by the maker.
6. Use the leftover batter to do the same.
7. Serve the waffles immediately with liked toppings or waffle sides.

Nutritional Values:

Calories: 100 g, Fat: 0.5 g, Carbs: 25 g, Protein: 2 g, Iron: 8.1 mg

Blackberry Pie

Bite into the iron rich blackberry pie to enjoy its tart delicacy. To fight with anemia this treat is tasty way to relish and revel in a classic dessert as it is loaded with rich antioxidants.

Prep Time: 20 min   **Cook Time: 35 mins + cooling**   **Servings: 8**

Ingredients:

80 ml quick-cooking tapioca (1/3 cup)	
720 g blackberries (4 cups)	
Dough for double crust pie	
28 g butter (2 tbsp)	
1.25 g salt (1/4 tsp)	
200 g sugar (1 cup)	

Instructions:

1. Take a pot, add Sugar, tapioca, & salt in it.
2. Add a cup of blackberries and combine together.
3. Tend to for fifteen mins or till the berries burst and the liquid gently boils, cook and stir the mixture at a moderate flame.
4. Mix the remaining berries after eliminating from the heat.
5. Set the temperature of oven at 400 F/200 C.
6. Make half of the dough to a round shape thick on a lightly dusted surface, then move to pie plate.
7. Trim it. Then, add the filling and butter the remaining dough into a circle that is 1/8 inch thick.

8. Put it over the filling. Trim the edges, seal it and flute.
9. Make cuts in the top. Bake for thirty-five to forty mins, till the top is golden brown.
10. Place it aside to cool then serve.

Nutritional Values:

Calories: 524 g, Fat: 26 g, Carbs: 69 g, Protein: 5 g, Iron: 2 mg

Chocolate Protein Balls

The delicious chocolate protein balls are the ideal anemia friendly dessert as they fulfil your sweet desire and offers you the amazing blend of enriched chocolate flavour. Every bite carries iron powered bliss.

Prep Time: 10 min **Cook Time: 00 mins + chilling** **Servings: 12**

Ingredients:

240 g raw cashews (1 cup)	
60 g sesame seeds (1/4 cup)	
200 g medjool dates (1 cup)	
30 g cacao powder (2 tbsp)	
225 g pumpkin seeds (1 cup)	

Instructions:

1. In a food processor, mix the seeds & nuts till they are crumbly.
2. Add cacao and dates. Process till the dry ingredients is combined with the seeds & nuts and a sticky crumb is formed.
3. When pushed between the fingertips, the mixture ought to hold together.
4. Make balls out of spoonful's of the mixture.
5. Consume the protein rich balls after cooling.

Nutritional Values:

Calories: 195 g, Fat: 12.88 g, Carbs: 13.4 g, Protein: 6.6 g, Iron: 2.7 mg

Cinnamon Sugar Pie Crust Cookies

Enjoy the happiness of munching while making stable your iron levels, it's a feast that truly fulfils everything. Experience the scrum sugar and cinnamon tastes and give your body a flurry of iron.

Prep Time: 15 min   Cook Time: 13 mins   Servings: 3 dozen

Ingredients:

120 g granulated sugar (1/2 cup)	2 unbaked pie crusts
45 g brown sugar (3 tbsp)	12.5 g ground cinnamon (2 ½ tsp)

Instructions:

1. Set the temperature of oven at 350 F/ 180 C.
2. Wrap the dish with parchment paper.
3. Start rolling out pie crusts on the dusted surface of 12*18-inch rectangle size.
4. Take a bowl, mix all the ingredients in it.
5. Sprinkle half mixture over the pie crust rolls.
6. Press the mixture in the pie crust rolls using hands and tightly cove the corners.
7. Firmly roll out the pie crust and start making thick cookie slices from the crust.

8. Adjust these cookies on the baking sheet. Transfer into the oven.
9. Start baking for fifteen mins till cookies top turn brown.
10. Serve these cookies with your favourite toppings.

Nutritional Values:

Calories: 210 g, Fat: 7 g, Carbs: 30g, Protein: 20 g, Iron: 2.8 mg

30-Day Meal Plan

	Breakfast	Lunch	Dinner	Dessert
1	Iron Rich Smoothie	Steaks With Goulash Sauce and Sweet Potato Fries	Garlic & Herb Steak Pizza	Chocolate Waffle
2	Tropical Green Smoothie	Mini Lamb Roasts with Balsamic Vegetables	Mediterranean Pork and Orzo	Double Chocolate Pancakes
3	Strawberry Banana Smoothie	Steaks With Goulash Sauce and Sweet Potato Fries	Spinach Dip in Bread Bowl	Chocolate Wafer Pie Crust
4	Anemia Fighting Smoothie	Sweet Teriyaki Beef Skewers	Grilled Garlic Butter Shrimp	Shoofly Pie
5	All-Natural Smoothie Bowl	Chickpea, Spinach and Egg Curry	Contest-Winning Greek Pasta	Chocolate cake
6	Breakfast Slice	Vegan Lentil Stew	Spicy Beef and Bell Pepper Stir-Fry	Easy Chiffon Pie

7	Cherry Cacao Smoothie	Mussels With Chorizo, Beans & Cavolo Nero	Grilled Chicken with Arugula Pesto	Chocolate Cream Pie
8	Vegan Pineapple & Coconut Baked Oatmeal	Lamb & Squash Biryani with Cucumber Raita	Shrimp Enchiladas	Fruit Cake
9	Chia Pudding	Oysters With Chili & Ginger Dressing	Crustless Ham And Collard Greens Quiche	Corn Custard
10	Eggs, Sriracha & Avocado Overnight Oats	Lentil & Beetroot Salad with Steak	Steak With Chipotle-Lime Chimichurri	Chocolate Pudding Pie
11		Chickpea, Spinach and Egg Curry	Chicken & Mushroom Puff Pastry Bundles	Frozen Hot Chocolate
12	Pumpkin Overnight Oats	The Ultimate Lamb Burger	Honey-Beer Braised Ribs	Cake Batter Dip
13	Lentils And Goat Cheese Toast	Mushroom & Tofu Stir-Fry	Grilled Salmon with Lemon Garlic Butter	Blackberry Pie

14	Overnight Steel Cut Oats	Sautéed Balsamic Spinach	Baked Beans with Ground Beef	Cinnamon Roll Waffles with Cream Cheese Glaze
15	Breakfast Quesadilla	Creamy Mushroom Steak	Angel Chicken	Cherry Cobbler
16	Chocolate Banana Oats	Penne With Eggplant, Tomatoes and Chick Peas	Quick Tacos Al Pastor	Rhubarb Pie
17	Kiwis And Spinach Smoothie	Sheet Pan Steak and Veggies	Caribbean Slow Cooker Pot Roast	Budin Puertorriqueno (Puerto Rican Bread Pudding) Recipe
18	Burrito Egg Casserole	Kale Quinoa Salad – With Lemon Dressing	Chicken Thighs with Shallots and Spinach	Tiger Nut Cake
19	Prune Juice Smoothie	Lentil Soup with Goat's Cheese Toast	Conga Lime Pork	Sour Cream Raisin Pie

20	Breakfast Sandwich	Pan-Seared Steak with Crispy Herbs & Escarole	Hawaiian Teriyaki Chicken Skewers	Easy banana cake
21	Kale & Quinoa Smoothie	Vegan Chickpea Tuna Salad	Creamy Fontina Cheese Pasta	Bacardi rum cake
22	Burrito Egg Casserole	Skillet Moussaka	Applesauce Pork Tenderloin	Spice Cake
23	Lenti Smoothie	Gochujang-Roasted Potatoes	Chicken And Vegetable Tagine	Honey Nut Oatmeal Waffles
24	Breakfast Sandwich	White Bean Soup	Hamburger Steak with Onions and Gravy	Blackberry Pie
25	Kale & Parsley Smoothie	Steaks With Goulash Sauce and Sweet Potato Fries	The Ultimate Pork Chops	Chocolate Protein Balls
26	Breakfast Quesadilla	Mini Lamb Roasts with Balsamic Vegetables	Easy Stuffed Flank Steak Pinwheels	Cinnamon Sugar Pie Crust
27	Avocado Toast	Skillet Moussaka	Beef And Swede Stew	Chocolate Waffle

28	Green Smoothie	Sweet Teriyaki Beef Skewers	Easy Slow Cooker Roast Beef Recipe	Double Chocolate Pancakes
29	Breakfast Slice	Lamb & Squash Biryani with Cucumber Raita	Cheeseburger Pizza	Chocolate Wafer Pie Crust
30	Dark Chocolate Smoothie	Vegan Lentil Stew	Garlic & Herb Steak Pizza	Shoofly Pie

Made in the USA
Monee, IL
07 November 2023

45944539R00111